JUSTICE FOR WOMEN:
THE NEED FOR REFORM

PRISON
REFORM
TRUST

The Report of the Committee
on Women's Imprisonment

Chaired by Professor Dorothy Wedderburn

First published in 2000 by the Prison Reform Trust

15 Northburgh Street, London EC1V 0JR

Copyright: Prison Reform Trust

ISBN: 0 94620 948 0 ✓

Designed and Printed by Advance Graphic Services,
Advance Works, 44 Wallace Road, London N1 2PQ.
020 7704 2236

Foreword

The number of women in prison has more than doubled in the last decade. Against that dramatic background the Prison Reform Trust commissioned this independent inquiry by Professor Dorothy Wedderburn and her colleagues.

Women in prison are people who the system has failed time and again: nearly half of them have been abused, over 40 per cent have self-harmed or attempted suicide, 20 per cent have spent time in local authority care and 36 per cent report having experienced serious problems at school. Yet over 70 per cent of women in prison have never experienced custody before.

It is timely that we should study these issues as plans progress for building two more women's prisons. In this report, Professor Wedderburn and her colleagues call for a radical rethink of sentencing policy as it affects women. They make a robust argument for an increase in the use of sensible alternatives to custody for women. They propose a dramatic revision of the way the Prison Service manages the women in its care.

Many women in prison are part of that group of socially excluded people about which we hear so much. It is for us to ensure that the criminal justice system strives to include them in society, rather than making them more isolated than ever.

It is my belief that this report makes an important contribution to that process.

The Rt. Hon. Lord Hurd of Westwell

Acknowledgements

When we began our work we were immediately struck by the willingness of both individuals and official bodies to share their expertise and experience with us. Without such help we could not have completed our task. We would like to record our thanks to them all.

The Prison Reform Trust took the initiative in commissioning this inquiry and was assisted in doing so by The Nuffield Foundation, City Parochial Foundation and the Eleanor Rathbone Charitable Trust. Bates, Wells and Braithwaite supplied resources in kind by allowing Mary Groom to act as joint secretary, and the Committee to meet at their convenient and agreeable offices.

We are particularly grateful to Linda Jones and her colleagues at the Women's Policy Group at the Prison Service for their help and support throughout our work. Chris Lewis and his colleagues at the Home Office Research and Statistics Directorate have also offered us invaluable assistance. We have drawn extensively upon their excellent published research reports.

A number of people met with us to discuss our progress and share ideas, and our thanks go to Louis Blom-Cooper QC, Silvia Casale, June McKerrow, Martin Narey, Joyce Quin MP, Sir David Ramsbotham and Viscountess Runciman.

Professor Andrew Ashworth at Oxford and John Braithwaite of the Research School of Social Sciences at the Australian National University supplied helpful comments on chapters 3 and 4, and Jenny Roberts at Hereford and Worcester Probation Service on chapters 5 and 6.

The seminars which we organised proved extremely valuable and we are indebted both to those who contributed such thoughtful papers, and to those who attended and participated in the lively discussions which took place in the pleasant surroundings provided by the Mental Health Foundation.

Two people who are not on the Committee, but who have contributed significantly to our work must also be acknowledged here. They are Toby Wolfe, who carried out research for us and Jenny Hughes, our sub-editor. In addition a number of staff at the Prison Reform Trust contributed time in typing, checking and proof-reading – Lucy de Lancey, Joe Levenson, Juliet Lyon, Margaret MacDonald, Liz Seward and Stephen Shaw.

Although we cannot name them individually, we would like to thank the governors and staff, members of Boards of Visitors, Probation staff and Education staff in the women's prisons for allowing us to visit and also for help and co-operation in talking to us.

Most particularly we are grateful to the many women prisoners who spoke to us about their experiences with great honesty and openness.

Finally members of the Committee wish to express their gratitude for the sterling work which our joint secretaries Clare Sparks and Mary Groom contributed over a much longer period than they originally envisaged.

Professor Dorothy Wedderburn

February 2000

Members of the Committee

Professor Dorothy Wedderburn – Formerly Principal of Royal Holloway and Bedford New College, Senior Research Fellow, Imperial College of Science, Technology and Medicine

David Faulkner – Senior Research Associate, University of Oxford, Oxford Centre for Criminological Research

Jane Geraghty – Deputy Chief Probation Officer, West Midlands Probation Service

Dr Chandra Ghosh – Consultant Psychiatrist, formerly Broadmoor Special Hospital, Medical Director, Pastoral Homes

Michael Goodwin (until Summer 1999) – Governor, HM Prison Service

Lesley Harvey – Vice-Chair, Board of Visitors, HMP Holloway

Professor Nicola Lacey – Professor of Criminal Law, London School of Economics

Elaine Player – Reader in Criminology and Criminal Justice, School of Law, Kings College, London

Wendy Rose – Senior Research Fellow, Open University

Lord Michael Mustill Kt, FBA, former Lord of Appeal joined the Committee but, after it began meeting, it became clear that his other commitments would prevent him playing an active role. He remained available for advice.

Co-Secretaries to the Committee

Mary Groom – Solicitor, Bates, Wells and Braithwaite

Clare Sparks – Policy Officer, Prison Reform Trust

"I lost everything. I lost – basically I lost friends… I lost my kids through it as well… At the end of the day, prison took my children from me, and nothing can ever repay for that. I lost everything – I lost the house, everything, do you know what I mean? It really did screw me up."

Former prisoner

Contents

Introduction

In February 1998 the Prison Reform Trust established a Committee to inquire into the use of imprisonment for women offenders and ways of reducing reliance upon custody. The terms of reference were deliberately widely drawn (**Appendix A**).

This move was prompted by concern about the rapid increase in the number of women in prison in England and Wales since the early 1990s (**Table 1**) and about the nature of the prison regimes under which these women were held in custody.

Table 1
Trends in the average prison population 1960-1998 (selected years)[1]

	Total prison population	Male population	Female population	Female population as % of total
1960	27,099	26,198	901	3.3
1965	30,421	29,580	841	2.8
1970	39,028	38,080	988	2.5
1975	39,820	38,601	1,219	3.0
1980	42,220	40,762	1,458	3.6
1985	46,233	44,701	1,532	3.3
1990	44,975	43,378	1,597	3.5
1995	50,962	48,983	1,979	3.9
1996	55,281	53,019	2,262	4.1
1997	61,114	58,439	2,675	4.4
1998	65,298	62,194	3,105	4.7

Why worry about women?

It may be argued that the number of women prisoners is still small compared with men (3,315 women and 61,964 men on 1 October 1999). So why pay particular attention to women? We realise that many of the considerations relating to penal policy which apply to women apply equally to men and some of our recommendations apply to all offenders irrespective of gender. But we also believe that the criminal justice and prison system is so dominated by the handling of men that it is failing to provide for the particular needs of women. This results in a system of treatment for women offenders which lacks both coherence and justification.

We have found four particular characteristics among women who enter the criminal justice system:

● First, the pattern of their offending remains very different from that of men and poses lower levels of risk to the public. Indeed, it has been argued that

---

1   Information provided by the Home Office.

even violent offences committed by young women tend to be less serious than those committed by young men.[2]

● Secondly, nearly half the women in prison had dependent children living with them at the time of imprisonment and were primarily responsible for the care of those children. This means that the imprisonment of these women has wider and longer term social repercussions, including costs to the state, than that of men.

● Thirdly, the adverse psychological consequences of imprisonment for women are more serious, not least because of the higher incidence of psychiatric morbidity among female prisoners and the adverse early life experiences of many of these women.

● Fourthly, the very fact that the number of women prisoners is relatively small presents serious logistical problems for their location and treatment. It results in many of them being held in prisons far from home and constrains the type of regime that can be provided.

Recent reports on women's imprisonment

Shortly before we began work, the report of the Chief Inspector of Prisons, Sir David Ramsbotham, *Women in Prison: A Thematic Review* was published by the Home Office. The aim of the *Thematic Review* was to help the Prison Service improve operating standards in prisons so that it could fulfil its Statement of Purpose.[3] It was wide ranging and, for the most part, critical of what it found. It contained no less than 160 recommendations. Some of these have been acted on by the Prison Service (though we have noted that there has been no official response to this important document in its entirety).

But Sir David's report was not, and could not by its nature have been, an overarching review of the criminal justice process as it applies to women. Although we echo many of his recommendations, we have tried to take a step back from the detailed considerations of the *Thematic Review* and to consider the principles (and some of the practices) that we believe should be applied to women's contact with the criminal justice system as a whole.

We have been aided in this task by the publication, during the period that we have been working, of four other extremely important documents:

● A review of community disposals and the use of custody for women offenders in Scotland, *Women Offenders – A Safer Way*, a joint report by the Chief Inspector of Prisons and the Chief Inspector of Social Work for Scotland, published by the Scottish Office (Edinburgh) 1998 (*Women Offenders – A Safer Way*).

● The results of an authoritative survey, entitled *Psychiatric Morbidity Among*

---

2 Rutter, M., Gillen, H. and Hagell, A. (1998), *Antisocial Behaviour by Young People*, Cambridge: Cambridge University Press. (See particularly Chapter 9.)

3 The Statement of Purpose is: *"Her Majesty's Prison Service serves the public by keeping in custody those committed by the courts. Our duty is to look after them with humanity and help them lead law-abiding and useful lives in custody and after release."* HM Prison Service 1999.

Prisoners in England and Wales, carried out in 1997 by the Social Survey Division of the Office for National Statistics on behalf of the Department of Health (*The ONS Survey*).

● A report of a joint working group between the Prison Service and the NHS Executive, entitled *The Future Organisation of Prison Health Care*, produced in March 1999 by the Department of Health (*The JWG Report on Prison Health Care*).

● A report of a Prison Service Working Group, with membership from external professionals and organisations as well as officials, entitled *Report of a Review of Principles, Policies and Procedures for Mothers and Babies/Children in Prison*, produced in July 1999 and available from the Women's Policy Group (*Report on Mothers and Babies*).

This last report is remarkable in that it calls for the Prison Service to play a leading role in influencing the consideration of non-custodial sentences as an alternative to imprisonment for women. The report has been welcomed by the Director General of the Prison Service. The Service's response, together with the Action Plan, was published in December 1999[4]. By and large we found the response both positive and comprehensive, but we await with interest the publication of the new Prison Service Order and Performance Standard under which Mother and Baby Units will operate.

Method of working

In our report we shall bring together the results of these disparate studies and of our own investigations. We have gathered evidence from a variety of other sources:

● We made an initial call for evidence from a wide spectrum of interested and knowledgeable people. A list of those who responded can be found in **Appendix B**.

● We have visited all but two of the establishments that hold women in England and Wales. A visit was also made to HMP Cornton Vale in Scotland. During each visit we made a point of meeting privately with prisoners and uniformed and other staff.

● Over the period of our work we have had regular meetings with members of the Women's Policy Group at HM Prison Service. We also met Sir David Ramsbotham, the Chief Inspector of Prisons, and Joyce Quin MP, then Prisons Minister.

● In January and February 1999 we held four seminars to which we invited various experts in their field. These seminars helped us to identify the main areas of concern. A list of those who attended can be found in **Appendix C**.

4   Available, by written request, from the Women's Policy Group and on the Prison Service website at www.hmprisonservice.gov.uk. The call to the Prison Service to seek to reduce the use of custodial sentences for women is rejected as being outside the Service's responsibilities. But attention is drawn to the fact that the Head of the Women's Policy Group is now responsible for *"leading on women in the Criminal Justice System in the implementation of the Home Office's Aim 4 'Effective execution of the sentence of the courts so as to reduce offending.'"*

- We commissioned a study by Toby Wolfe, an economist, entitled *Counting the Cost: the Social and Financial Consequences of Women's Imprisonment*, 17 February 1999.

The need for reform

> *This report will make the case for an urgent and radical reform of the arrangements for dealing with women offenders in England and Wales and of the extent to which they are imprisoned.*

There are many arguments about the social functions that imprisonment fulfils in modern western society. But, whatever the purpose, it is commonly agreed to be a system of punishment designed with men, rather than women, in mind. Women have been seriously disadvantaged by this process and the consequences are becoming more severe in the prevailing climate of criminal justice policy. As the official agenda focuses ever more sharply on the protection of the public from 'dangerous' offenders, it is becoming increasingly irrelevant to the realities of female offending and increasingly destructive in its effect - not just on women but on their children too. The costs of imprisoning women - for them, their children and society - are, as we have found, manifold and often long-lasting.

How a society deals with offenders is in part a matter of choice. A large number of options already exist but, for various reasons, are under-utilised. So we have sought to explore the principles which might guide that choice and to indicate the consequences for sentencing policy.

> *We will argue that for the most part women prisoners represent the extremes of social exclusion which present government policy is aiming to reduce, and that a logical addition to the array of policy proposals now flowing from the many government departments involved, would be one from the Home Office detailing the steps it proposes to take to reduce significantly the imprisonment of women.*

The structure of the report

To make our case we shall present this report in the following way:

Chapter 1

Examines trends in the number of women who are detained in prison, whether or not they are serving sentences. It analyses the pattern of offending, the characteristics of the offenders and the sentencing and remand policies which have resulted in these women being detained.

Chapter 2

Describes the present prison system and the nature of the prison experience for women.

Chapter 3

Examines the principles of punishment for offending which currently prevail and, finding them in important respects both limited and confusing, articulates those principles which should underpin society's response.

Chapter 4

Looks at the implication of these principles for sentencing policy.

Chapter 5

Reviews the variety of penalties already available to the courts and their evaluation to date. We look at how non-custodial penalties might be used with greater confidence and extended, and the nature of the regimes which it might be appropriate and practical to apply to women offenders.

Chapter 6

Suggests a new framework for penal practice for women which could integrate objectives of criminal justice with broader aims of social justice and inclusion.

Chapter 7

Summarises our recommendations and conclusions.

▌ The Female Prison Population

1.1   Proposals for reform must be developed within a policy framework that is based on the realities of female crime, within which the imprisonment of women is evaluated not just in the context of the criminal justice system but as a part of the present government's commitment to 'joined-up social policies for joined-up social problems'. We begin by looking at what is known about the characteristics of women's offending and the profile of women in prison.

Explaining the increase

1.2   In 1998 the average population of women in prison rose to a level that had not been seen since the end of the nineteenth century. Despite fluctuations since then - for example during wartime - the overall trend had been downwards to the extent that in 1970 there were only 988 women held in prison. This led to optimism about the effectiveness of treatment for female offenders and about the ability of non-custodial penalties to provide an adequate degree of public protection.

1.3   Such expectations were soon to change as faith in the rehabilitative ideal was replaced first by disillusion and then by a commitment to retributive justice. In the late 1960s women made up less than 3 per cent of the total prison population; on average fewer than 1,000 women were held in prison at this time (**Table 1**). Then, alongside the growth of the male prison population, the numbers of women in custody started to rise - slowly at first but from 1992, after the collapse of the liberal ambitions of the 1991 Criminal Justice Act, the numbers of men and women in prison increased sharply. The rate of growth was, however, most rapid for the female population which more than doubled in five years. The Home Office's own projections assume that this trend will continue. In the year ending July 1999, the total prison population actually fell but, within the total, the number of female prisoners continued to rise – from 3,190 to 3,260.

1.4   In assessing the extent of women's imprisonment it should be also borne in mind that the size of the prison population only measures the numbers of women in prison at a particular moment in time; as such it inevitably underestimates the sum total of those experiencing imprisonment over a period of time. In 1998 the average population of women prisoners was 3,105 but there were 10,100 receptions of women prisoners into custody during that year.[5]

Offending and the imposition of penalties

1.5   In order to understand this rapid increase it is necessary first to examine

---

5   Some women will, of course, have been received more than once. But the total number of receptions within a year far exceeds the total number in custody at a point of time.

rates of offending and then to attempt to unravel the complex process of dealing with offenders through the various stages of the criminal justice system. There are difficulties in doing this, not least because the reporting and recording of crime can be influenced by many extraneous factors. But over long periods, and given broad similarities between advanced industrial countries, general trends can probably give a good indication. An authoritative study has concluded that:

"The post war period has witnessed a general pattern of rising crime rates which have been a pervasive phenomenon in most Western countries"[6]

although it is suggested that the trend is less clear cut in the last few years. There is also some evidence that, at least among juveniles, the rate of female offending has risen faster than the rate of male offending.[7]

1.6   There is no simple correlation between rates of offending and rates of imprisonment because many stages in the criminal justice system intervene (we discuss these in **Chapters 4** and **5**). Here we concentrate on those who, for one reason or another, end up in prison. A statistical analysis by the Home Office of the extraordinary growth of the female prison population between 1992 and 1996 suggests that it is the result of the interaction of three factors:

- an increase in the number of women appearing before the courts;
- an increase in the proportion of those women receiving a custodial sentence;
- an increase in the length of prison sentences being imposed on these women.

The Home Office analysis concludes that between 1993 and 1996 the major cause of the rise was a shift in sentencing practice by the Crown Court. Half of the growth was due to an increase in the courts' use of custody for women appearing before them and a further 20 per cent was due to an increase in average sentence lengths.[8] The numbers of women appearing before the Crown Court also went up during this time and accounted for the remaining 30 per cent of the increase. Between 1996 and 1997, 95 per cent of the increase in women prisoners could be accounted for by an increase in the numbers appearing before the courts. It is interesting to compare this picture with the comparable picture for men, where 63 per cent of the increase in the male prison population can be attributed to an increase in custody rates, only 12 per cent to the numbers sentenced and 26 per cent to an increase in sentence lengths[9].

1.7   The Home Office analysis also shows that 50 per cent of the female population increase between 1993 and 1996 was explained by an increase in the numbers of convictions for drug offences.[10] Other serious categories of offence also played a part. Violence against the person accounted for 14 per cent of the population growth, and offences of robbery, theft and handling stolen goods explained 10 per cent each. Between 1996 and 1997 the influence of drug

6   Rutter, M. et al (1998), op. cit. p.69.
7   Rutter, M. et al (1998), op.cit. p.74. This applies to juveniles.
8   Woodbridge, J. and Frosztega, J. (1998), *Recent Changes in the Female Prison Population*. London: Home Office.
9   Throughout this report, percentage figures may not total 100 per cent because of rounding.
10 Drugs offences include trafficking, possession and possession with intent to supply. The category does not include drug-related crime e.g. property offences committed to support a drug habit.

offences continued to rise, explaining 68 per cent of the growth, while domestic burglary and criminal damage explained 18 per cent and 12 per cent respectively. This pattern of convictions goes a long way to explain the overall increase in sentence length because drug offences tend to attract significantly longer sentences than most other categories of crime. For example, in 1997 the average sentence for a drug offence was 30 months compared with 10 months for theft.

1.8   Over the last few years claims have been made that women are now receiving more severe treatment than men in the criminal justice system. As far as custody is concerned there is little evidence to support this view. On the contrary an authoritative Home Office study concluded that all the evidence pointed the other way. Of women aged 21 and over sentenced in the Crown Court a lower proportion than for men were sentenced to immediate custody for each type of indictable offence and the average length of sentences for women was also shorter.[11]

1.9   Home Office work also points out that although, overall, women offenders may be dealt with more leniently than men, this does not rule out the possibility that individual women may receive unduly harsh treatment. Indeed there are other studies which strongly suggest that women whose lives do not conform to prevailing ideas of appropriate female roles, and whose offences violate those stereotypes, receive relatively harsh treatment.[12] Further work to analyse sentencing patterns is needed.

The remand population

1.10   It is impossible to consider the rise in the female prison population without paying special attention to those remanded in custody. Women held on remand awaiting trial or sentence represent a substantial 20 - 25 per cent of the total female population. And even these figures underestimate the impact that this category of prisoners has on the daily work of the Prison Service. In 1998, there were 10,100 receptions into the female estate, 6,258 (62 per cent) of which were women held on remand.[13] In keeping with the growth of the sentenced population, the average number of unconvicted and unsentenced women held in prison increased by 18 per cent in the same year.[14] This population is weighted towards the unconvicted; almost three-quarters of women remanded in custody are awaiting trial whilst only a quarter are convicted women awaiting sentence.

1.11   It is obviously important to understand how such a substantial number of women who have not been convicted and sentenced come to be held in prison, when the average time spent awaiting trial is over four weeks and when ultimately a significant proportion (as many as a fifth) will be acquitted.[15]

11   Home Office (1997i), *Aspects of Crime and Gender 1997*, London: Home Office Research and Statistics Directorate.

12   Other relevant studies by the Home Office are :- Hedderman, C. and Hough, M. (1994), *Does the Criminal Justice System treat men and women differently?* Home Office Research Findings 10; Hedderman, C. and Dowds, L. (1997), *The Sentencing of Women, a section 95 publication*, Home Office Research Findings 58; Hedderman, C. and Gelsthorpe, L. (1997), *Understanding the Sentencing of Women*. Home Office Research Study 170; Flood-Page, C. and Mackie, A. (1998), *Sentencing Practice: An Examination of Decisions in Magistrates Courts and the Crown Courts in the mid 1990s*, Home Office Research Study 180 (1998); Home Office (1999iv) *Women in the Criminal Justice System; a section 95 publication*, London: Home Office Research and Statistics Directorate.

13   Home Office (1999i), *Prison Statistics England and Wales 1998*, Table 1(e).

14   Ibid, Table 2.1

15   Home Office (1999i), op.cit. Table 2.6.

1.12   Do women held on remand possess distinctive characteristics? In so far as we are concerned with the nature of their 'offences', the answer by and large is no. The offence profile of women held on remand is similar to that of women in prison who have been sentenced (**Table 2**) except that 'drug offences' feature more prominently for the sentenced.

Offence Group	Remand%	Sentenced%
Violence against the person	16	18
Theft and handling	27	17
Robbery	6	7
Burglary	7	5
Drug offences	23	34
Fraud and forgery	3	5
Other offences, including sexual offences	17	10
Offences not recorded	3	5
TOTAL PERCENTAGE	100	100

Table 2
Female remand and sentenced prison population by offence group 1998.[16]

In fact the offences which figure more prominently for the sentenced group are not surprisingly those which attract the longer sentences.

1.13   In so far as we are concerned with the personal characteristics of women on remand, as distinct from sentenced women, the answer by and large is yes; they are distinctive, particularly in respect of their mental health and drug use. The *ONS Survey* provides probably the most comprehensive comparison of the characteristics of remand and sentenced women prisoners, since that distinction was a major classificatory variable in much of the data analysis. While it appears that the two groups have had similar experiences of deprivation, there is some suggestion that women on remand may have experienced greater turbulence in their lives (being expelled from school, for instance, or having been homeless.)[17]

1.14   However, it is in relation to mental health problems that the biggest differences are to be found. Although the same percentage of both groups, 40 per cent, had received help or treatment for a mental health problem before entering prison, more remand prisoners had been admitted to a mental hospital and they were twice as likely to have been admitted to a locked ward or secure unit.[18] While the prevalence of 'personality disorder' was high in both groups, the probability of psychosis and of neurotic disorders was greater among the remand population. Furthermore, women on remand appear to be at a high risk of suicide. Over a quarter had attempted to kill themselves in the last year and nearly a quarter had had suicidal thoughts in the previous week.

1.15   A further disturbing characteristic of the female remand population is the prevalence of drug use. Of most concern was the ONS finding that opiate dependence - either alone or together with dependence on stimulants - was particularly common amongst the women on remand, who were also the group of prisoners most likely to have used drugs intravenously.

16   Ibid Tables 1.5 and 2.8.
17   Singleton, N. et al (1999), op.cit. Table 16.3.
18   Ibid Chapter 8.

1.16   These data prompt a number of disturbing questions. Is it possible that the courts lack sufficient evidence of the situation of some women when they come before them to feel confident enough to pass sentence immediately or to use their powers to divert? Or do they make a presumption, simply from evidence of deprivation, drug taking or mental ill health that such women would be unreliable in answering bail? We shall return to these questions in **Chapter 5**. In this chapter, we need simply to draw attention to the numerical importance of this category of women prisoner and note that to be in prison on remand - if only for a relatively short time - can disrupt family life and cause deep distress just as much as being held under sentence.

The criminal profile of women in prison

Type of offence

1.17   In the offence profile of the sentenced women held in prison there has been a significant shift since 1993 because of the rapid increase in drugs offences (**Table 3**).

Table 3
Female population in prison under sentence by offence group.[19]

Offences with immediate custodial sentence, women.	1993	1994	1995	1996	1997	1998
Total number	1,125	1,266	1,456	1,727	2,063	2,366
	%	%	%	%	%	%
Violence against the person	19	22	20	20	19	18
Burglary	4	3	4	5	5	5
Robbery	7	7	7	7	8	7
Theft and handling	18	18	19	18	16	17
Drug offences	27	26	27	28	34	34
Fraud and forgery	6	5	6	7	6	5
Fine default	2	2	2	(0.3)	(0.1)	(0.04)
Other offences, including sexual offences	12	11	10	10	9	10
Offences not recorded	6	7	6	4	3	5
TOTAL PERCENTAGE	100	100	100	100	100	100

1.18   It is difficult without a great deal more information to judge the degree of seriousness of the offences committed by women in prison. In the face of the recent media attention given to violence by young women, it would be helpful to be able to say something about the nature of their offences as they are grouped under the broad headings of the criminal statistics. Violent crime, for example, includes violence against children but also pub fights and attacks on abusive partners. It is worth noting that only about a quarter of the women received into prison for violence against the person in 1998 received sentences of more than 12 months (only 41 women in all were sentenced to more than four years

19   Home Office (1999i), op. cit. Table 1.7. Percentages may not add up, due to rounding

in prison, including 12 who received life). As for drug offences, data supplied to us by the Home Office shows that half of the 691 women in prison for these offences in June 1997 had been convicted of illegal importation/exportation; a further fifth was convicted of unlawful supply; another fifth with intent to supply and the remainder (7 per cent) for possession. These categories cover a wide spectrum of criminal behaviour, from major entrepreneurial dealing through to low-value trading to support a personal drug habit.

1.19   But notwithstanding the increased numbers of women prisoners convicted of these serious categories of offence, the reality is that they still only account for a minority of the women who receive a prison sentence. Violent offences, robbery, burglary and drug offences together accounted for just under a third of all receptions under sentence in 1998. The most common crimes for which women were being sent to prison that year were still theft and handling stolen goods which, together with offences for fraud and forgery, accounted for almost half (48 per cent) of the 4,778 sentenced women received that year.[20] Concern which is often expressed about the numbers of women in prison who have been convicted of violence should be balanced by the recognition that a similar number of women will be entering the prison system because they have been convicted of a motoring offence, a public order offence (such as drunkenness and threatening or disorderly behaviour) or because they are in breach of a previous court order.

Chart 1
Female and male receptions under sentence, 1998

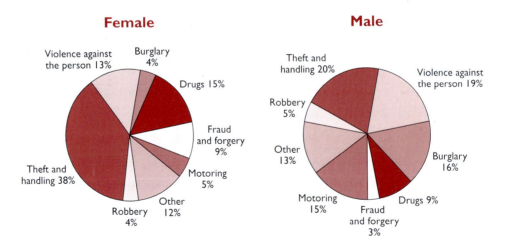

Female

Violence against the person 13%
Burglary 4%
Drugs 15%
Fraud and forgery 9%
Motoring 5%
Other 12%
Robbery 4%
Theft and handling 38%

Male

Theft and handling 20%
Violence against the person 19%
Robbery 5%
Other 13%
Burglary 16%
Drugs 9%
Fraud and forgery 3%
Motoring 15%

---

20   Ibid, figure 4.10.

Chart 2
Sentenced female prison population, 30 June 1998

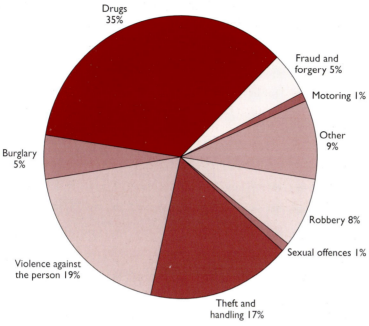

Length of sentence

1.20   While it is difficult without more information to draw conclusions about the degree of seriousness of the offences committed by women, some indication of how those offences have been viewed by the courts can be found in the figures on length of sentence. The reality is that the vast majority of women received into prison are serving very short sentences: in 1998, 55 per cent of the women received under sentence were serving six months or less and, more than three-quarters, 12 months or less.[21] Women serving sentences of more than 18 months are a small minority and, given the present arrangements for early release, most women will actually stay in prison for only one half of their sentence.[22] In consequence, there is a rapid movement of women through the prison system, so that only about a quarter of those now being received will stay for longer than six months.[23] We argue later in this chapter (**1.27 – 1.29**) that even a short period in prison is disproportionately disruptive for women and their families.

1.21   More than one third of women in prison on any day have no previous convictions and only 20 per cent have seven or more. These figures are in contrast to those for the male population, where 15 per cent have no previous conviction and 44 per cent have 7 or more.[24] The majority of women in prison are there for the first time and the majority of women released from custody are unlikely to receive another conviction within two years after their release. This is

---

21   Home Office (1999iv), op.cit.

22   Those prisoners sentenced before 1 October 1992 are eligible to be considered for parole at the one-third point in their sentence and if they are not granted parole they will be released unconditionally at the two-thirds point. If parole is granted, prisoners are released on supervision to the probation service until the two-thirds point. For those sentenced after 1 October 1992, different rules apply. Prisoners serving less than four years are automatically released at the half-way stage of their sentence. Prisoners serving over four years become eligible to be considered for release on parole at the half-way stage.

23   Even when all determinate sentenced prisoners are considered, the average stay of those discharged in 1997 was 10.5 months.

24   Home Office (1999i), op.cit. Table 4.2.

interesting evidence in the light of the currency now given to the idea that women in prison have been given endless chances by the courts and are a highly recalcitrant recidivist population.

1.22   None of this is to deny that there are some women in prison who have committed serious offences and have caused harm to their victims. What we do argue, however, is that these women represent a small proportion of all those entering the prison system. This is not a novel or perverse reading of the evidence; it is a conclusion which other commentators have commonly drawn:

> **"..most women sentenced to imprisonment are non-violent offenders and many have committed minor offences"**[25]

> **".. less than 1% of female convictions are for violent offences and very few of the women sent to prison are violent offenders. A significant number of women imprisoned for relatively petty offences are first offenders".**[26]

> **".. a greater proportion of women could be held without physical security restrictions as they do not represent a danger to the public".**[27]

1.23   To summarise, there can be little doubt that women are less likely to commit crimes than men, they are less likely to commit serious crimes and their offending careers are shorter.[28]

> **Our conclusion from this review is that the majority of women entering the prison system do so without having committed a serious offence and without being a risk to the safety of the public.**

This alone must raise questions about whether, and how far, prison is an appropriate sentence for them. In addition it is necessary to take into account their social background and the social consequences of removing them from the community.

Personal characteristics

1.24   As a result of the recent studies referred to in our Introduction, we can now discern a much clearer and more accurate picture of the background of women in prison. We find that they are overwhelmingly, although not exclusively, drawn from a group who share all the characteristics of 'social exclusion'. As

25 Penal Affairs Consortium (1996), *The Imprisonment of Women: Some Facts and Figures.* London: Penal Affairs Consortium.

26 Social Work Services and Prisons Inspectorates for Scotland (1998), *Women Offenders - A Safer Way: A Review of Community Disposals and the Use of Custody for Women Offenders in Scotland,* Edinburgh: Stationery Office.

27 HM Chief Inspector of Prisons (1997i), *Women in Prison – a thematic review,* p.20.

28 Rutter, M. et al (1998), op cit. p.260.

children they have experienced a wide range of adverse circumstances and events, such as parental separation, periods in local authority care, interrupted education and various other forms of disadvantage.[29]

1.25   The majority of women prisoners are young and have dependent children. Only 16 per cent are over 40 and amongst the 50 per cent who are under the age of 30 there is an increasing number of young offending women under the age of 21. In 1998 they numbered 333 and of most concern is the fact that 1 in 5 of these were juveniles, aged between 15 and 17, who could more properly be described as children.

1.26   More than 60 per cent of women in prison are mothers and 45 per cent had children living with them at the time of their imprisonment. Whatever the sex of the prisoner, imprisonment has a disruptive impact on the family. But the effect, particularly on children, is most acute when it is their mother, rather than their father, who is imprisoned. We estimate that the living arrangements of more than 8,000 children are affected each year as a result of their mother's imprisonment. It is often claimed that the real numbers are higher than this because some mothers do not reveal that they have children for fear that they may be taken into local authority care.[30]   One recent study has shown that in 8 per cent of cases the women's children were placed in local authority care as a result of their mother's present imprisonment.[31]

1.27   The problems which women have in making alternative living arrangements for their children, and in coping with the breakdowns in these arrangements during their sentence, figure constantly as a major preoccupation and cause of anxiety among women prisoners. A Home Office study of imprisoned mothers revealed the very young age of the children that women prisoners leave behind: almost a third of the children were under the age of five and two-thirds were under 10.[32]   For the vast majority (85 per cent) the current period of custody was the first time that the children have been separated from their mothers for any significant length of time.

1.28   The longer term disruption that is caused to the families of imprisoned women is illustrated by the increased number who expect to live as lone parents on their release and by the finding that 10 per cent of the women who lived with their children before coming to prison do not expect to do so after release.[33] Furthermore, the same Home Office study found that half the mothers nearing release were not expecting to return to their previous accommodation, almost four out of 10 had lost their homes and there was an increase in the number expecting to be homeless. Research which examined the post-release experience of women prisoners found that the women's situation was generally worse than had been expected.[34]   Women frequently discovered that their children had been experiencing problems which no one had told them about whilst they were in prison; accommodation turned out to be more unstable and

---

29   For ongoing analysis of the way in which childhood experience of poverty, family disruption and contact with the police is linked to adverse adult outcomes, see the important work of the Social Exclusion Centre at LSE, in particular, Hobcraft, J. (1998), *Intergenerational and Life Course Transmission of Social Exclusion*. Working Paper 15 and Kiernan, K. (1999), *Childhood Poverty, Early Motherhood and Adult Social Exclusion*. Working Paper 28.

30   For a full assessment of the evidence see Wolfe, T. (1998), *Counting the Cost: The Social and Financial Consequences of Women's Imprisonment*, London: Prison Reform Trust, p.18.

31   Ibid, p.15.

32   Caddle, D. and Crisp, D. (1997), *Imprisoned Women and Mothers*, Home Office Research Study 162, London: Home Office.

33   34 per cent lived as lone parents prior to imprisonment, 43 per cent anticipated doing so prior to release. Caddle, D. and Crisp, D (1997), op. cit. p.50.

34   Morris, A., Wilkinson, C., Tisi, A., Woodrow, J. and Rockley, A. (1995) *Managing the Needs of Female Prisoners*, London: Home Office.

unsatisfactory, financial problems and debts were more serious and finding employment was more difficult.[35]

1.29   In the light of the link between teenage pregnancy, early motherhood and social exclusion, which is emerging from the work of the LSE Centre for the Analysis of Social Exclusion and the Cabinet Office Social Exclusion Unit, we should not be surprised that women prisoners tend to have given birth to their first child at a much earlier age than women in the general population. More than half (55 per cent) of the women in the survey of imprisoned mothers had given birth in their teens in comparison with 20 per cent of the general population. Imprisoned women were also three times more likely than women in the general population to be lone mothers; 27 per cent compared to 8 per cent.[36]

1.30   It is significant, in view of the evidence of a cycle of deprivation, that more than a quarter of the women themselves had been in care as a child. One of the most interesting findings to emerge from the LSE studies, at least from our point of view, has been the discovery of a gender difference in the effects that being in local authority care can have on subsequent adverse experiences as adults:

> **"Girls who were in care or fostered were particularly likely to have had extra-marital births, three or more live-in partners, become teenage mothers - and - experience(d) several other negative adult outcomes (homelessness, lack of qualifications and low household income)... Boys seem less vulnerable to negative consequences of care or fostering...This gender difference in the effect of care as an antecedent to adult exclusion is dramatic."[37]**

1.31   The *ONS Survey*, in particular, suggests that almost all the women had suffered at least one stressful life event and almost half had experienced at least five. The most common were running away from home, serious money problems, separation or the breakdown of a steady relationship, the death of a close relative or friend .[38]

1.32   Typically, their education record was poor, with two out of every five women having left school prematurely. Only 3 per cent had been in employment before coming into prison and over half reported that they were living on state benefits. But it was the evidence produced about the extent of violent and sexual abuse suffered by many of the women, both as children and as adults, that was most shocking. The *ONS Survey* found that half the women reported having suffered violence at home and one in three women reported sexual abuse. Identical results were produced in the *Thematic Review*, which emphasised the fact that, for the most part, the abuse suffered by these women had occurred in

35   Ibid p.34-35.

36   Caddle, D. and Crisp, D. (1997), op. cit. p.11.

37   Hobcraft, J. (1998), op.cit. p.91.

38   Singleton, N. et al (1998), op.cit. *Summary Report*, p.27.

their domestic environment and had been inflicted by men close to them, such as their fathers and partners.

1.33   The extent of the deprivations experienced by women prisoners before conviction has been well documented in all the recent studies. It should also be remembered that the distressing pictures they present relate to experiences that have been packed into the relatively short life spans of young women.

Mental health

1.34   The prevalence of mental disorder amongst the female prison population has long been recognised and for many years confirmed the 'mad rather than bad' reputation of women offenders. The full extent of psychiatric problems within prisons has, however, only recently been reliably established.[39]

1.35   The *ONS Survey* revealed that the prison population, both male and female, displayed far higher rates of mental disorder than any other nationally surveyed population, including the general population and the population of homeless adults. Almost one in five women prisoners had spent time as an in-patient in a mental hospital or psychiatric ward and as many as 40 per cent reported receiving help or treatment for a mental, nervous or emotional problem in the year before coming into prison. Half the women interviewed were taking some form of medication acting on the central nervous system, 'particularly hypnotics and anxiolytics and anti-depressants'.[40] A sub-sample of women who were clinically assessed revealed a high incidence of functional psychosis, neurotic symptoms and personality disorder. As much as half the population was diagnosed as suffering from a personality disorder, a third being assessed as having an 'anti-social' personality disorder. Rates of self-harm are alarmingly high among both women and men prisoners. The *ONS Survey* established that 7 per cent of male sentenced and 10 per cent of female sentenced prisoners had harmed themselves during their present prison term while 34 per cent of sentenced women compared to 20 per cent of men had entertained suicidal thoughts within the last year.

1.36   A large proportion of all prisoners were found to have several mental disorders but the prevalence of functional psychosis, such as schizophrenia and manic depression, and neurotic symptoms and disorders was notably higher for female than male prisoners. However, it was amongst women remanded in custody, as we noted (**1.15**), that the highest rates of disorder were detected. We shall discuss the implications of this in more detail in **Chapter 2**, where we look at existing conditions for women in prison, and in **Chapter 5**, where we look at alternatives to custody.

Clearly a major question for public policy must be the extent to which prisons should be used to accommodate people with mental health problems.

39   Maden, A., Swinton, M. and Gunn, J. (1994), 'A Criminological and Psychiatric Survey of Women Serving a Prison Sentence' *British Journal of Criminology* 34 (2); Singleton, N. et al (1998) op cit.

40   Singleton, N. et al (1998), op. cit. p.25.

Drug use

1.37   In this review of the personal characteristics of women in prison, we must examine what is known about the degree and nature of substance misuse. The position revealed by the Inspectorate's *Thematic Review* has been closely reflected in the *ONS Survey*. This showed that a large majority of women prisoners had used illicit drugs at some time in their lives and that almost half reported a measure of dependence on drugs in the year before coming to prison.[41]   Poly-drug use was common but a larger proportion of women than men were dependent on opiates and a substantial number of these women reported intravenous use. The survey exposed a clear correlation between certain property offences and drug dependence:

"In general, both men and women held for burglary, robbery and theft had above average rates of drug dependence before coming to prison."[42]

The rise in the number of women serving sentences for drug offences, the shift towards longer sentences, and the correspondence between substance dependency and property crime all point to the significance for women prisoners of illicit drugs and of the heavy penalties imposed on drug users.

1.38   In introducing these data, however, we must take account of the presence in prison of a substantial number of foreign national women. These women made up no less than 15 per cent of the population in 1998 and, of them, 71 per cent had been convicted of drug offences and were serving significantly longer sentences than their British counterparts.[43] In 1997, 58 per cent of the foreign national women convicted of drug offences were sentenced to more than four years in prison compared with only 15 per cent of the British nationals.[44] The length of these sentences means that these women pose particular problems for the management of prisons, as well as experiencing great hardship themselves. Their ignorance of the British criminal justice system makes it difficult for them to deal either with solicitors or with prison staff. They do not have access to bail facilities or - in the case of those subject to a deportation order at the end of their sentence - to open prisons at the end of their sentence. The difficulties which British women experience in maintaining contact with their families are multiplied many times over. Foreign national women face additional problems of distance and cost in keeping in touch, and they are frequently isolated within the prison by language and cultural barriers. Given that substantial numbers of them will be deported at the end of their sentence, their position must raise important questions about the purpose which imprisonment is expected to fulfil in these cases.

1.39   The presence of this number of foreign national women is also relevant to understanding the heavy over-representation of prisoners of 'black' ethnic origin in the female prison population as a whole. Almost 1 in 5 female prisoners

41 Singleton, N. et al (1998), op. cit. p.21.

42 Singleton, N. et al (1998), op. cit.

43 Home Office Research and Statistics Directorate, letter to Committee dated July 2 1999.

44 Home Office Offenders and Corrections Unit, letter to Committee dated 17 September 1998.

is categorised as 'black' (meaning that they are of African or Caribbean origin) which is a much higher representation than is found in the male prison population. But 52 per cent of the overseas nationals are classified as 'black'. If they are excluded from the statistics the proportion of black British nationals is reduced to 12 per cent.[45] This is still over-representation when compared to the general population in the relevant age groups. But these women also tend to be serving relatively long sentences because they have been convicted of drug offences which, as we have seen (1.8), are dealt with more severely by the courts. Half of the 'black' British nationals are in prison for drug offences (which incur longer sentences) compared with only a quarter of 'white' British nationals.

* * * * * * * * * * * * *

1.40   Finally, it is relevant at this point to ask whether changes in wider social and economic conditions over the last 20 years or so could have contributed to the number of women being imprisoned. We know that persistent poverty has increased markedly over the last quarter of a century. Today a third of all children live in households with incomes below the official poverty level, and are persistently poor.[46] Other characteristics of 'social exclusion' as the government defines it have been increasing in incidence. There is, of course, no simple correlation with offending. We do not subscribe to any simplistic view of the causes of offending among women. Not only are there a number of women in prison who have not experienced such a combination of deprivations, but for those who have it is still possible to escape from the patterns and tendencies involved.[47]

1.41   However, as we stated at the beginning of this chapter, proposals for reform must be based on the realities of female crime. Sentencers must be aware of the life experiences of the women who come before them for whom prison represents a culmination. What does imprisonment do for them? In the next chapter we review the experience of prison for women.

---

45 Home Office Research and Statistics Directorate, letter to Committee dated 2 July 1999.
46 HM Treasury (1999), *The Modernisation of Britain's Tax and Benefit System No. 4 - Tackling Poverty and Extending Opportunity*, London: Home Office.
47 Hobcraft, J. (1998) op cit. p.95.

2 The Prison System For Women

2.1 Our terms of reference (**Appendix A**) asked us to consider various aspects of the women's prison system such as its structure, the rules and regulations under which women's prisons are run and the treatment of mothers and babies.

2.2 Visits by members of the Committee to fourteen prisons holding women were an important part of the work we undertook. These confirmed and, for us, brought to life the general findings of authoritative studies such as Sir David Ramsbotham's *Thematic Review* (and his subsequent reports on particular prisons) and the *Report on Mothers and Babies*. Some members of our Committee had never been inside a prison and were shocked by the conditions which they found. All of us subscribe to the view expressed by Pat Carlen that:

> **"overwhelming evidence of the mismatch between the present state of women's prisons and the needs of the women currently being sent to them is already available."**[48]

2.3 We cannot hope to improve on her picture of the nature of the prison experience, or that provided by Angela Devlin who published her account of what is wrong with women's prisons shortly after we began work.[49] What we shall do in this chapter is to comment on certain structural aspects of the women's prison system which most markedly underline the disjunction between what imprisonment appears to be intended for and the ability of a system, designed predominantly for men and taking no account of the distinctive features of women's patterns of offending and needs, to deliver. We shall also comment on some welcome signs of change that are beginning to appear in the way the Prison Service is approaching this dilemma.

The establishment

2.4 There are 125 prisons for men in England and Wales and 16 prisons holding women. The total annual cost of the women's estate is £67,359,555 (5 per cent of the total annual expenditure). The average cost in 1998 - 1999 of a place in a women's local prison was £27,426 (men £24,604) and in an open prison £16,995 (men £14,505).[50]

2.5 Because of the relatively small number of women's prisons, women are more likely than men to be held at a considerable distance from home and in locations which are both costly and difficult to access. This in itself creates great

48 Carlen, P. (1998), *Sledgehammer: Women's Imprisonment at the Millennium*, London: Macmillan, p.ix.
49 Devlin, A. (1998), *Invisible Women*, Winchester: Waterside Press.
50 HM Prison Service (1999), *Annual Report and Accounts April 1998 - March 1999*, London: Home Office.

hardship for the significant proportion of women who are primary carers of children or other relatives. Keeping in touch with family and friends can be particularly hard, while the need to do so is often particularly strong.

2.6   This issue is further complicated by the fact that the women's prisons are not evenly spread around the country. The south is dominated by Holloway which holds over 500 women (that is about one in six of the total number of women prisoners) and acts as a local prison. The north of the country is dominated by Styal which has undergone refurbishment so that it is now of a similar size to Holloway. Apart from Eastwood Park, near Bristol, there is no other prison serving the south-west of the country so that women from Devon and Cornwall, for example, are likely to have to travel the considerable distance to Eastwood Park or Holloway. There are no women's prisons in Wales. To the west of the Pennines, there is no women's prison north of Cheshire.

2.7   There are only three open prisons for women in the country - at Askham Grange near York, East Sutton Park in Kent and Drake Hall in Staffordshire. For women serving sentences in open prisons the chances of being placed near home are, therefore, especially remote.

2.8   With the exception of Holloway, women's prisons have been adapted from other uses - such as military camps, male prison establishments and manor houses - which has the effect of constraining regimes; in some cases they provide only dormitory accommodation. Some new provision has recently been made available for women, and the Prison Service plans to build at least two new prisons for women over the next three years. This may make some difference, but it seems that the majority of women will still find themselves in establishments far from home and difficult to access for visitors.[51]

Current pressures

2.9   Women's prisons are operating under great pressure. There are several factors which currently exacerbate the situation:

- First, overcrowding - this applies in varying degrees and (despite the re-provision) to all prisons. For example the female annexe at Winchester was once a 66 room long-term training prison for women serving over 2 years. It now holds 94 women serving between 2 months and 25 years. As a result the authorities have had to resort to housing these women three to a room.

- Secondly - this also applies to all prisons - prison budgets for staff and other resources are based on a prison's Certified Normal Accommodation (CNA). A prison may operate - and most are operating - at their 'Operational Capacity' which may be 10 - 20 per cent above CNA. There will normally be no increase in staff or other resources in response to the excess population over CNA.

---

51   In view of the thrust of our argument, namely that the numbers of offending women being given custodial sentences or placed on remand can be reduced without risk to the public, this use of scarce capital resources to build additional places for women must be regretted.

- Thirdly, there is (as with all public services) a requirement for the Prison Service to reduce unit costs (or to deliver "cost improvements") normally by 3 per cent per annum. This has placed governors under constant pressure particularly in relation to staffing levels.

Because the rise in the number of female prisoners has recently been steeper than the rise in male prisoners, these three factors are tending to bear more heavily on the women's system.

There is also an additional factor that bears only on women:

- Much of the new female accommodation provided in recent years has been converted from male establishments often at short notice and with insufficient attention paid to its appropriateness for women or to the training of staff. Within the last three years Highpoint, Send, Low Newton, Foston Hall and Brockhill have been at least partially converted and Durham has had another female wing added to the existing high security H wing.

Changing from male to female use

2.10   The process of converting prisons has not always been successful, not least because of the speed of the changeover compounded by the need to change the attitudes and practices of staff. All prison officers we spoke to emphasised how different it was to work with women.

2.11   The changes at Highpoint in Autumn 1996 and at Brockhill in 1998 were particularly difficult. The Inspectorate comments that the change of use from male to female at Highpoint was *"tackled without informed co-ordinated advice and support from the Prison Service"*.[52] It also comments that Brockhill's governor and staff *"were left to carry out the conversion without co-ordinated support and advice from the Prison Service"*.[53] Indeed the most recent Inspectorate report on Brockhill still comments that it is important that there should be *"the right attitude among all staff realising that Brockhill is now a women's local prison and not a male Category C training prison"*.[54]

2.12   Conversion has caused particular difficulties in terms of security and most particularly searching. The Inspectorate has commented that at Highpoint *"the prison has fewer female officers than it needs for supervision and particularly for searching"*.[55] It recommends that 75 per cent of staff in female prisons should themselves be women as, quite rightly, male prison officers are not able to search female prisoners. The rapid change of use of some prisons has resulted in there being insufficient numbers of female staff to carry out these duties.

2.13   Women's prisons also require special training for staff - a fact which was emphasised to us by staff themselves. Training for work with women has generally been very limited. The Trust for the Study of Adolescence was commissioned by the Prison Service to produce a training pack entitled

---

52   HM Chief Inspector of Prisons (1997ii), op. cit..
53   HM Chief Inspector of Prisons (1997i), op. cit.
54   HM Chief Inspector of Prisons (1999), HMP Brockhill - Report of a Full Inspection.
55   HM Chief Inspector of Prisons (1997ii), op. cit..

Understanding and Working with Young Women in Custody which has received high acclaim.[56] But, as it is not compulsory, it has taken some time to reach all the women's prisons. Additionally training involves releasing staff from normal duties - never easy in the environment of a rising population and, for staff in the prisons concerned, opportunities have been still further restricted by handover problems.

The structure

2.14   Until April 1998 policy affecting women had been dealt with together with policy affecting young offenders. At that point, the Prison Service established a Women's Policy Group at Prison Service Headquarters. This is the first time in 25 years, despite the distinctive and pressing needs of women prisoners, that specific provision has been made to consider the issues. The remit of the Women's Policy Group is, eponymously, a policy-dominated one, with no line management responsibility and a limited budget. Nonetheless since its formation the Group has been extremely active and brought welcome improvements. An example of the positive work which has been undertaken is the *Report on Mothers and Babies*. It contains many positive proposals which, in its Response, the Prison Service has said will be incorporated in the new Performance Standards. We welcome this although, as with all such Standards, it is the monitoring of their implementation which is all important.[57] Governors have expressed appreciation that members of the Policy Group have made efforts to visit them and to listen to the views of staff. The importance of research has been recognised and some has been undertaken. The attempt to change the ethos and to take a strategic look at the women's prison system as a whole has figured high on the agenda.

2.15   We welcome the new responsibility assigned (December 1999) to the Head of the Policy Group for leading on the role of women in the criminal justice system. This development is part of the Prison Service's contribution towards realising the Home Office's Aim 4: *"effective execution of the sentences of the court so as to reduce re-offending and protect the public"*.[58]

2.16   To date, the control of resources still runs from the centre of the Prison Service through the area managers to the prison governors. But, as from December 1999, it has been announced that there will be an Operational Manager for Women's Prisons. We welcome this as a first step – although we shall argue (**Chapter 6**) that there is need for a more far-reaching reform of the structure.

Regimes

2.17   The combination of overcrowding, restricted budgets and attempts at cost improvement is damaging further the quality of many regimes. In the course of our visits we heard many reports of cuts, particularly in services provided as

56   Lyon, J. and Coleman, J. (1996), *Understanding and Working with Young Women in Custody*, HM Prison Service Training Pack. Brighton: Trust for the Study of Adolescence.

57   See footnote 4.

58   Home Office (1999), *Protecting the Public, The Correctional Policy Framework*, London: Home Office, p.3.

outside contracts which are the easiest to cut. Thus the education and probation services tend to be worst hit. But discipline staff are also under acute pressure resulting, for example, in unacceptable restrictions on time spent out of cell. On our visits we learned of a number of cases where women had been locked up from Saturday midday until Monday morning. The *ONS Survey* showed that one in four female sentenced prisoners had spent more than 19 hours in their cell on the previous day.[59] Given the background of many of the women in prison, and given the nature of their offences and their personal difficulties, the bearing of these restrictions on the amount of constructive and/or therapeutic work that can now be done in women's prisons is particularly unfortunate.

2.18   New money has recently been made available to the Prison Service through the Government's Comprehensive Spending Review. Women's prisons have gained £22.57 million for drug treatment work nationally and £25.75 million for regime development. Simultaneously Holloway and Styal have been allocated an additional £500,000 per prison per year for three years in order to enable them to develop enhanced regimes for women. While this additional finance is to be welcomed, it is (a) earmarked and (b) ad hoc. So it cannot seriously contribute to a systematic development of programmes designed to serve the needs of women prisoners.

Health care

2.19   Health care, as we have already seen (**1.35 – 1.40**), is a central need of women in prison, in view of the large numbers who have - or have experienced - mental health problems and/or are - or have been - misusing drugs. But there is also strong evidence of poor physical health.[60]

2.20   Provision of health care in prison is the responsibility of the Prison Service, not of the National Health Service. The arrangement for delivery varies from prison to prison, influenced by the particular custodial function of the institution, by the policies pursued by individual governors and by history. In 1994 health care standards were promulgated with the overall aim of giving prisoners *"access to the same quality and range of health care services as the general public receive from the NHS"*.[61] But there have been criticisms that these standards have not been consistently enforced or even monitored leading to a growing number of calls for the service to be incorporated wholly within the NHS.[62]

2.21   The report of a joint Prison Service and NHS Working Group published in 1999 (*The JWG Report on Prison Health Care*) reviews the present situation and presents a critical account which coincides with the more superficial impression gained on our own visits:

*"**Health care in prisons is characterised by considerable variation in organisation and delivery, quality, funding, effectiveness and links with the NHS"**.*[63]

59 Singleton, N. et al (1998), op. cit. Table 15.1.
60 Ibid, table 4.9.
61 HM Prison Service (1994), *Health Care Standards for Prisons in England and Wales*, London: Home Office.
62 For example see the list of recommendations (which in this case stop short of a call for transfer of responsibility to the NHS) in HM Chief Inspector of Prisons (1997) op. cit.
63 HM Prison Service (1999) *The Future Organisation of Prison Health Care*, London: Home Office, para 6.

2.22   In women's prisons health care expenditure as a percentage of the total budget varies from just over 5 per cent to 20 per cent, and per capita of the average daily population from £1,200 to £7,000 with an average of £5,000.[64] There are, of course, compelling reasons for some variation but as long as decisions about medical staffing levels and overall medical expenditure remain the responsibility of individual governors, and in the absence of clearly defined clinical standards, it is difficult to see how change will be achieved.

2.23   In the course of our visits we were made aware of the extent to which women's prisons fail to distinguish clearly between custodial and health functions, both in terms of roles and of the skills required of staff. We also observed the practice, and its undesirable consequences, of calling upon health care centres to manage prisoners who fail to cope on prison wings.

2.24   Sadly the JWG Report on Prison Health Care failed to make recommendations for any change in overall responsibility for health care in prisons, but proposed a five-year programme of formal partnership between the Prison Service and the NHS. To oversee the joint working, there is to be a Task Force (established in September 1999) to help prisons and their relevant Health Authorities develop Health Improvement Programmes at local level, consistent with those being planned by Health Authorities for their local communities, and then to oversee the implementation of the required changes. A further integrating body is proposed, a Prison Health Policy Unit to replace the current Prison Service Directorate of Health Care. Its responsibility, as its name implies, would be for the development of national policy and for advising both Home Office and Health Ministers. It will be located in the NHS Executive in the Department of Health.

2.25   These proposals may improve things. But the Government's published Response to the JWG Report can only be described as lukewarm in the light of the pressing need for major improvements in the delivery of health care to women prisoners.

The facts in Chapter 1 indicate, consistent, reliable state-of-the-art health care for women prisoners is a matter of extreme urgency.

The use of prescribed medication and the availability of treatment for drug and alcohol misuse are the most outstanding issues where change is essential.

The pattern of medication

2.26   It may seem strange to isolate medication as an issue but there is much evidence to suggest that a comprehensive audit of patterns of drug prescribing in prison is overdue and should, particularly for women, be tackled urgently. We are told that data on prescribing histories of individual prisoners are no longer centrally collected (and this at a time when the NHS is devoting increasing resources to analysis and feedback in the community generally).[65]   Experts argue that women's prisons use outmoded (and themselves addictive) drugs in unacceptable dosages where modern alternatives are available, albeit at somewhat greater cost.[66]   In this way prison treatment itself is liable to perpetuate or even increase addiction. We do not know whether this state of affairs is the consequence of prison medical staff being out of date, being negligent or being constrained by lack of resources or whether it reflects lax prescribing by GPs before the woman entered prison.

> **But we recommend urgently the undertaking of an audit of drug prescribing in prison and the development, in collaboration with the NHS, of a protocol for prescribing for women prisoners which should be monitored by NHS personnel.**

Drug and alcohol misuse

2.27   There is no doubt that drugs are a major cause of women being received into prison and a major source of concern in women's prisons. (**Chapter 1** and **Charts 1** and **2**). Despite official attempts to exclude drugs from prison and the use of Mandatory Drug Testing (MDT), 34 per cent of female sentenced prisoners had used drugs in their current prison term.[67] A recent official review of the policy of MDT in prisons found that any deterrent effect was principally among cannabis users whereas we know that it is opiate addiction which is particularly prevalent among women prisoners. Moreover the review could find no evidence that MDT had succeeded in directing drug misusers into treatment. Nonetheless it concluded that the programme had achieved its objectives and no change was recommended. The MDT programme consumes a great deal of staff time, thereby limiting the time available for activities which might promote rehabilitation, as well as causing resentment and in some cases humiliation among women prisoners. MDT remains part of the Prison Service Drug Strategy. However with the additional resources made available after the Comprehensive Spending Review (see **2.18**) new initiatives are being developed. Therapeutic communities are being established at two women's prisons, residential rehabilitation units at a further two and voluntary drug free testing units in all prisons. Finally all prisons are involved in a new programme which spreads over into follow-up in the community, post-release (Community Assessment Referral Advice and Treatment Service – CARATS). These are most welcome programmes, but the scale of the drug problem is such that, in our view, they require far more resources to be devoted to them.

---

65   Hansard Written Answer. 25 May 1999. Column 75.

66   Professor Robert Kerwin, Professor of Clinical Neuropharmacology at the Institute of Psychology in paper to Conference *The Crisis in Women's Prisons*. Research Centre for Violence, Abuse and Gender Relations, Leeds Metropolitan University, June 1999.

67   Singleton, N. et al (1998), op.cit. Table 9.12. The data do not distinguish foreign nationals although it should be noted that the prevalence of drug dependence in the year prior to entering prison of sentenced women prisoners was lower among the 'black' ethnic group (24 per cent) than among the 'white' ethnic group (46 per cent) - table 9.16.

> **We would challenge the view that drug treatment regimes in prison are adequate for the situation.**

For it is not just the drugs themselves, or even the disciplinary problems that direct access to them produces, that are the only problem. They also give rise to bullying and attacks on those prisoners thought to possess a supply by those desperate to access it.

* * * * * * * * * * * * *

2.28   We now comment on three other major features of life in women's prisons which illustrate how provision within the women's system fails to meet their specific needs: prison visits, temporary release (as affected by general security measures) and sentence planning.

Prison visits

2.29   During the 1980s and early 1990s, the importance of social ties for all prisoners, male and female, was acknowledged when improvements were made in the arrangements for prison visits generally. For women prisoners these ranged from financial assistance for relatives on low incomes to the extended all-day visits at Holloway and Styal enabling children to visit their mothers in a more informal setting. In 1991, following the Woolf Report, the minimum entitlement of one visit per month was doubled for all prisoners to one a fortnight.

2.30   But the geographical dispersion of the women's estate and the increase in the number of women in prison no doubt account for the finding in a Home Office study that only half the women who had lived with their children or been in contact with them before imprisonment had seen them since coming into prison.[68] Many governors were aware of this undesirable development and some attempted to compensate for this by operating a more liberal policy of home leave. But these initiatives were brought to an abrupt end in April 1995 when a more restrictive system of temporary release was introduced to address problems of home leave failure in the male system. We have been pleased to learn that most recently steps have been taken to return to a more liberal regime for visits but staffing levels remain a serious constraint.

Temporary release

2.31   The escape of male prisoners from two high security dispersal prisons, Whitemoor and Parkhurst, prompted a major review of prison security in the mid-1990s. The conclusions of the Woodcock Inquiry into

---

68   Caddle, D. and Crisp, D. (1997), *Imprisoned Women and Mothers*, Home Office Research Study 162, London: Home Office.

the security breaches at Whitemoor, and the recommendations of the wider ranging security review by Sir John Learmont into the escapes from Parkhurst, set off an escalation of security which was to affect all categories of Prison Service establishment.[69] For women, it meant a restriction of temporary release which was to be governed henceforth by rules drafted with high security male prisoners in mind.

2.32   The 1994 Home Office study of imprisoned women and mothers found that children's needs were the main reason for home leave applications. The curtailment of temporary release has meant that women who were previously granted home leave in order to be present at a child's hospital appointment or first day at school, or as part of a resettlement programme, have had these privileges withdrawn. The Chief Inspector in his *Thematic Review* expressed concern about the blanket application of the new rules on temporary release and recommended that there should be

> ***"a special review of the criteria for the eligibility for temporary release as applied to women prisoners".***[70]

2.33   The impact of the Woodcock and Learmont reports, combined with an increasingly punitive approach to criminal justice, has also led to other wide-ranging and damaging consequences for women prisoners. Dedicated search teams, introduced primarily as a response to the firearms, explosives and drugs smuggled into HMP Whitemoor, were set up in women's prisons, with the consequence that strip-searching increased. Women were more routinely handcuffed on visits to outside hospitals or to attend other appointments concerning their family. This eventually captured public interest when the handcuffing of a woman in labour was widely reported in the press. The practice was condemned by the Chief Inspector of Prisons:

> ***"...the increased focus on security ... has placed unwarranted restrictions on women under escort. The vast majority of women are not an escape risk, nor do they pose serious danger to the public."***[71]

More recently the Prison Service bowed to public pressure and issued an instruction to all governors that:

> ***"... women admitted to NHS hospitals to give birth should not be handcuffed from the time of their arrival until they leave."***[72]

2.34   Pat Carlen has detailed the litany of harmful and degrading consequences for women in her description of the 'new punitiveness' and 'fetishism of prison

69   Home Office (1994), *The Escape from Whitemoor Prison on Friday September 1994* (The Woodcock Inquiry) cm 2741 London: Home Office; Home Office (1995), *Review of Prison Service Security in England and Wales and the Escape from Parkhurst Prison on Tuesday 3rd January* (The Learmont Inquiry) cm 3020, London: HMSO.

70   HM Chief Inspector of Prisons (1997i), op. cit. Para 8.23.

71   HM Chief Inspector of Prisons (1997i), op. cit. Para 5.21.

72   H.M. Prison Service (1997), Circular Instruction 5/97.

security' in the 1990s. Central to her argument are two conclusions. The first is that the new focus on prison security causes an additional punishment to be imposed on women prisoners that is inappropriate and irrelevant to the risks they represent. Secondly, the way in which these measures are imposed has different meanings and significance for women which may exacerbate the punitive effects. Carlen, for instance, discusses the ways in which some women perceive and experience strip-searching in prison:

> **"...although accepted as an inevitable and justifiable part of prison life by many prisoners, [strip-searching] is seen as a violation of personal autonomy and modesty by others, especially those who have never taken drugs, who have suffered sexual abuse, are from countries where feminine modesty is rigorously enforced or who already agonise over their body shape. To these latter groups of women strip-searching can cause deep distress and, in some cases, provoke extreme acts of resistance to what is experienced as an assault."**[73]

Sentence planning

2.35   The women's prison system, due in part to its small size, has traditionally provided a scaled-down range of educational and training opportunities in comparison to those offered in most male training prisons. The small number of prisons holding women, alongside the Prison Service's commitment to housing women as close to home as possible, means that establishments are required to fulfil a multi-functional remit rather than focus on one aspect of provision.

2.36   Yet there are a growing number of women in prison who are staying for increasing lengths of time. For them, it can be argued, prison holds out the possibility of rehabilitative opportunities through education and vocational training. In recent years there has been a resurgence of interest in 'offending behaviour programmes' designed to tackle the causes of certain types of criminal behaviour. But, until recently, the focus of these has tended to be on the most serious categories of male offending, namely sex offender treatment programmes and anger management courses for men convicted of impulsive and serious violent crime. More recently, welcome initiatives have also begun in the women's system. For example, Styal is developing a course for female sex offenders and a regime for women with severe mental health problems. The Prison Service Drug Strategy has also provided a new emphasis on treatment programmes for those with problems of substance dependence (although, as we indicated in **2.27**, the scope of these programmes remains inadequate).

2.37   In general, women serving medium and long term sentences do not have opportunities for sentence planning equivalent to those available to male

---

73   Carlen, P. (1998), op.cit. p.7.

prisoners. From our own observations when visiting women's prisons, the educational and training possibilities appeared limited in scope and impoverished of resources. The main criticism of education in women's establishments made by the Prison Inspectorate was:

"...the absence of an overall assessment of the educational and vocational needs of the prisoner population and a policy to identify the role education services are expected to play in women's prisons."[74]

Yet we know a great deal about 'needs' already (**Chapter 1**). We know about the poor levels of literacy and numeracy, the relatively truncated experiences in the school system and the dearth of skills that could lead to employment. Furthermore, many teachers and other staff emphasise how important it is for women who lack self-esteem and have histories of failure within formal education to experience a degree of achievement, however modest, during their time in custody. We agree with this view. But we believe that there is a limited amount that can be achieved for the majority of women who are serving six months or less.

2.38   Further, the role of education in offering women a legitimate route towards reshaping their own lives (whether through qualifications and skills training, by generating greater awareness about such things as health care, child care, or financial management or by inspiring them with new interests that will enrich their leisure) is most obviously frustrated when it will cease once the woman returns to the community. Without a community base and the prospect of longer-term involvement, to believe that education facilities in prison will offer women any real chance of change is to place hope above experience. This is a major consideration which points us towards the view that conventional prisons can have only a small contribution to make to the appropriate treatment of women offenders (**Chapters 5** and **6**).

Perpetuating social exclusion

2.39   The present Government is committed to policies which are designed to tackle poverty, to extend opportunity and, in its own words, to reduce "social exclusion".[75] It has placed great emphasis on the need to understand the multiple factors (and their interaction) which influence people's trajectories through life. It has promised to identify the extent to which social and economic policy initiatives must be consonant if they are to be effective. But these reforming measures will take time to improve the position of the socially excluded. Meanwhile there is a pool of both men and women who will remain untouched.

---

74   HM Chief Inspector of Prisons (1997i), op. cit.

75   Social exclusion is defined by the Government's Social Exclusion Unit as *"a shorthand term for what can happen when people or areas suffer from a combination of linked problems such as unemployment, poor skills, low income, poor housing, high crime environments, bad health, poverty and family breakdown"*.

2.40   We have studied, so far as time would allow, the work now being carried out by the Centre for Analysis of Social Exclusion at the London School of Economics. This convincingly concludes that social exclusion is transmitted across the generations and through the life course (whilst recognising that there is *"huge scope for many, if not most, individuals to escape from the pattern and tendencies observed."*[76]) In drawing together the material in our first chapter we have been struck by the similarity between the characteristics of so many of the women in prison now and the characteristics which Hobcraft and Kiernan have identified as being the strongest predictor of adverse adult outcomes, in other words social exclusion.[77] Moreover, because the data we present in Chapter 1 documents the disruption which children suffer as a result of their mother's imprisonment, the evidence provided by Hobcraft *"as to the extent and pervasiveness of both specific and general continuities across the generations"* is completely relevant.[78]

2.41   The financial costs to society are explored in the work which we commissioned from Toby Wolfe.[79]

> **Here we wish to make the more significant point that a government seriously concerned to pursue measures to reduce social exclusion and improve 'adverse adult outcomes' cannot ignore the repercussions from the criminal justice system, as it currently operates, upon other social policies.**

These considerations too, as well as those put forward above, point to the need for the exploration of forms of punishment other than prison for women offenders.

✳ ✳ ✳ ✳ ✳ ✳ ✳ ✳ ✳ ✳ ✳ ✳ ✳

Before we make practical recommendations, however, we must pause to consider the rationale for our social response to women offenders and, indeed, the conditions under which it is legitimate for the state to punish any offenders, men or women, particularly by imprisonment.

---

76   HM Treasury (1999), op.cit.
77   Hobcraft, J. and Kiernan, K. (1999), op.cit.
78   Hobcraft, J. (1998), op. cit. p.96.
79   Wolfe, T. (1998), op.cit. See Appendix D.

3 A Principled Approach

Why we need to justify punishment

3.1   In previous chapters, we have set out facts about women's offending and current penal practice in relation to women. Clearly, these facts should inform the practical recommendations for the reform of the treatment of women in the criminal justice system for which the rest of this report will argue. But they can only do so by way of a set of moral and political principles – by way, also, of an account of the rationale for our social response to offenders and of the conditions under which it is legitimate for the state to punish offenders.

3.2   At first glance, this question of justification might be thought too obvious to merit discussion in a special section of a report such as this. After all, the vast majority of citizens support the institution of state punishment and, though levels and forms of punishment excite political controversy, the basic practice of punishing appears more or less beyond question. Yet there are several reasons to think that we should be clear about the principles by which we can justifiably punish.

Because we have choices

3.3   First, punishment by the State is costly in both human and financial terms and its practical advantages are often uncertain. The very fact that we have come to take it for granted makes it incumbent on us to question the moral basis on which our practices are founded.

Perhaps one of the most important preconditions for any reasoned public debate about penal policy is the recognition that a society has choices - often hard choices - to make about forms and levels of punishment. This is sometimes obscured by the recognition that individual decisions about punishment are for the courts rather than politicians. Yet legislative intervention in the sentencing system, the longstanding executive involvement in practices such as early release from prison, and the recent decision to appoint a Sentencing Advisory Panel to advise the courts on principles of sentencing all implicitly recognise the fact that there are collective - indeed political - choices to be made.

It is crucial to recognise that these choices include decisions about how many of our limited public resources should be devoted to the costly practice of punishment as opposed to other social policies such as education, employment, health and housing - each of which may have important practical implications for crime.

Because we need 'joined-up' policies

3.4   Secondly, the controversies about proper forms and levels of state punishment which surface regularly in political debate cannot themselves be analysed except in terms of some broader view of the rationale for the criminal justice system. For example, any argument for a reduction in the use of imprisonment or for the introduction of a new penalty, such as the electronic curfew, takes place against the backcloth of more general views about the functions of criminal justice and about the proper limits of state power.

* * * * * * * * * * * * *

This chapter therefore begins by setting out some general principles on which legitimate criminal justice policies need to be based. It then moves on to consider the main justifications advanced for state punishment, drawing out those principles which resonate most loudly with contemporary practice in Britain and considering whether, in their terms, women are receiving equitable or appropriate penal treatment. Through this discussion, we also identify a number of limitations in the framework informing contemporary penal practice and go on to argue for a revised set of criminal justice principles.

How we may justify punishment

3.5   We may base an adequate justification for punishment on:

Citizenship

3.5.1   Ideally, the principles governing state punishment would appeal to values widely shared across society. But in the real world of diverse societies, such consensus is generally unattainable. However, we will set out from a very general proposition which we assume to be relatively uncontroversial in contemporary Britain: that criminal justice practices should be designed so as to recognise and respect the rights and responsibilities of all members of the community to the greatest degree which is compatible with a similar respect for others. In short, punishment must be compatible with the basic ideals of citizenship in a liberal and democratic society.

Consistency

3.5.2   The goals and values informing criminal justice practice should be consistent with those informing other important areas of social policy. Thus although the specific context of criminal justice may be expected to pose its own distinctive political and moral demands, a penal practice which flew in the face of other valued social aims, such as the aim of minimising social exclusion, would be vulnerable to objection.

Equity

3.5.3   Principles of punishment should be such as to be capable of being applied in an equitable and non-discriminatory way to members of different social groups. We assume, in particular, that the same general principles of punishment should be applied to men and women. But the equitable treatment of women and men does not in itself imply equal treatment in a literal sense.[80] Rather, equity is to be understood in terms of treatment as an equal. Hence facts such as those canvassed in **Chapter I** - facts about the social context of women's offending and about specificities in patterns and forms of women's offending - are of direct relevance to a proper penal policy for women. Most obviously, to the extent that women offenders present lower levels of social danger - both qualitatively, in the sense of the seriousness of the crimes they commit, and quantitatively, in terms of their levels of offending and likelihood of re-offending - this would imply substantially different treatment for women in the penal system.[81] The same implication arises, conversely, from evidence that the social costs of imprisoning women are in significant respects higher than those of imprisoning men.[82]

3.5.4   Perhaps more controversially, the idea that penal practice should cohere with other social values suggests that on occasion facts such as those canvassed in previous chapters may actually affect the legitimacy or at least the proper extent of state punishment. For example, if a large proportion of certain groups of offenders are people whose basic citizenship rights - such as the right to physical or sexual integrity - have been violated by abuses from which the state has failed to protect them, this must be a relevant factor in determining the nature, if not the fact, of their punishment.[83] Similarly, at a yet more basic level, where an offender has received less than their fair citizenship share of public resources such as education, this should affect the state's investment in the educational or other relevant aspects of their sentence. Though criminal justice creates its own moral imperatives, these can never be entirely insulated from broader questions of social justice.

The standard rationales for punishment

3.6   Standard rationales for punishment divide broadly into two groups:

Desert-based approaches

3.6.1   The first set of arguments may be described as backward-looking or retributive and have the merit of appealing to common sense: they advance the idea that punishment should be proportional to the offenders' deserts, and that proportional punishments are required by justice. Retributive arguments have moved on from the ancient *lex talionis* which spoke in terms of 'an eye for an eye' and today argue - consistently with modern notions of human responsibility - that the measure of punishment should reflect not only the gravity of the harm

---

80   Carlen, P. (1998), op. cit.

81   See 1.19 – 1.20.

82   Wolfe, T. (1998), op. cit.

83   Hudson, B. (1998) 'Mitigation for Socially Deprived Offenders', in A. Von Hirsch and A. Ashworth, (eds) *Principled Sentencing*, Oxford: Hart Publishing, p.205.

or wrong done by an offender but also the degree of his or her culpability in doing it.[84]   Nonetheless, the modern theory of just deserts shares one key feature with the ancient approach to retribution; in looking exclusively backwards to the offence, each implies that there is some intrinsic moral worth in the practice of punishment whether or not it has any further beneficial social consequences which cancels out its *prima facie* wrongfulness.

Goal-based approaches

3.6.2   The second set of arguments are forward-looking or consequence-oriented and start out from the idea that punishment is *prima facie* an evil and must be justified by compensating good effects.[85]   Specific goals include: the deterrence of actual offenders through the experience of punishment or the general deterrence of potential offenders through fear of punishment; the incapacitation of offenders in the name of public protection; the use of punishment as an occasion for reform or rehabilitation. Broader objectives may include punishment as a potentially socialising or formative institution whose effects go beyond mere deterrence or coercion to the inculcation of shared community values enshrined in criminal law.[86]

Strengths, weaknesses

3.6.3   Unfortunately, these general principles of punishment are notorious for telling us rather little about exactly what form punishment should take. Views differ as to what desert requires: the calculation of actual or probable consequences of punishment is difficult to assess. This means we can get only limited help from the two 'pure' retributive and utilitarian approaches to punishment when we seek to shape the principles which should govern the use of imprisonment. But a focus on the specific question of imprisonment suggests that the forward-looking approach appears to have one advantage over its retributive rival. Clearly, either principle has to take into account the uniquely intrusive, stigmatising, psychologically painful and expensive attributes of imprisonment as a penalty. Yet while on the forward-looking approach, the deterrent, rehabilitative, incapacitative and other effects of imprisonment can in principle be measured, the relation between a certain prison term and a certain level of culpability or desert is subject to no metric. Notwithstanding the strong commitment of desert theorists to the parsimonious use of punishment, therefore, desert approaches in practice tend to be particularly vulnerable to swings in popular or political reaction to crime.

3.6.4   On a more general level, the strengths and weaknesses of each of these approaches mirror those of the other. While desert-based approaches appear to offer certain prescriptions about the proper scale of punishment, and fit with certain pervasive moral intuitions, the suspicion remains that to impose punishment irrespective of beneficial social consequences is a form of vengeance. Conversely, the consequence-oriented approach to punishment, while its cost-

84   For a modern statement of desert theory, see Von Hirsch, A. (1976) *Doing Justice: The Choice of Punishments*, New York: Hill and Wang. Von Hirsch's more recent and sophisticated statement is to be found in his *Censure and Sanctions* (1993) Oxford: Clarendon Press.

85   The classic statement of this approach is to be found in Jeremy Bentham's utilitarian philosophy: see Bentham, J. (1983, first published 1789) *An Introduction to the Principles of Morals and Legislation*, London: Methuen.

86   See Braithwaite, J. (1989), *Crime, Shame and Reintegration*, Cambridge: Cambridge University Press.

benefit principle would appear to be transparent and efficient, does not help us much with the distribution or quantum of punishment. Why not punish an innocent person if the deterrent consequences would outweigh her suffering? Why not merely pretend to punish if this would achieve deterrence without incurring cost? Why not threaten draconian penalties for trivial offences if this would effectively prevent them? Finally, in their most common forms, each of the pure theories tends to ignore the interaction between criminal justice and broad questions of social policy and social justice: how far is an offender's just desert for crime affected by broader social injustice? May the short-term and direct pursuit of policies of crime reduction through increased punishment turn out to be counter-productive in the longer term and in the light of broader policy objectives?

3.6.5   These complementary strengths and weaknesses mean that penal policy in real social orders rarely reflects a purely desert-based or consequence-oriented approach. Yet ideas about rationales of punishment incontrovertibly inform government policy and penal practice. It seems important therefore to focus on those ideas which currently express themselves in criminal justice practice.

The current framework – and are women fairly treated within it?

3.7   The prevailing rationale for punishment in Britain is a somewhat uneasy mix of desert- and goal-based considerations. The Criminal Justice Act 1991 introduced a general principle that punishment should be commensurate with the seriousness of the offence except in a limited range of cases where the offender's dangerousness justified a longer sentence. But, due to a combination of legislative, judicial and broadly political factors, the general principle has become substantially diluted by concerns about deterrence and incapacitation.

3.8   Nonetheless, it can be argued that even on the basis of the rather opaque principles implicit in contemporary policy, the current levels of women's imprisonment are inappropriate and unjustified :

- It is sometimes assumed that the rapid increase in the female prison population may be justified in terms of the increasing dangerousness of women offenders. Yet this argument is contradicted by the facts about women's offending. The claim appears to amount to an attribution of a global disposition of 'dangerousness' rather than a rigorous assessment of the likelihood of serious reoffending. The distinctive pattern of female offending analysed in **Chapter 1** undermines any generally incapacitative argument for an increased population of women prisoners.

- Equally, a careful study of the facts about women's offending undermines the argument that there is untapped potential for deterrence through increased severity.[87] On the contrary, the typical social context of female offending

---

87   For a review of the literature on deterrence, see Von Hirsch, A. Bottoms, A. Burney, E. and Wikstrom, P.O. (1999), *Criminal Deterrence and Sentencing Severity: An Analysis of Recent Research*, Oxford: Hart Publishing.

makes such an assumption particularly inapposite.

- The long-term effectiveness of incapacitative custodial sentences is particularly open to question in relation to women.[88] Since the vast majority of the female prison population is released into the community within a relatively short space of time, the disruptive effects of imprisonment in terms of personal and employment relationships, housing and so on suggest that the long term effects of imprisonment are counter to the interests of public protection.

- It is important not to lose sight of the fact that the social costs of penal severity reach well beyond the pecuniary costs of prison sentences. There is strong reason to think that the disruptive effects and indirect costs of imprisonment are especially high for women.[89] This is so not least because social structures which still accord women primary responsibility for domestic labour and child-rearing, along with the growing number of female-headed households, mean that the practical and emotional implications of a woman's imprisonment for her family are often devastating. The effect on the intergenerational transmission of social exclusion is of particular concern.[90]

3.9   We therefore believe that the current levels of imprisonment of women cannot be justified, according to the best available evidence, on any of the goal-based rationales implicit in prevailing practice.

3.10   We would argue that current levels of imprisonment of women are disproportionate as well as inefficient. In this we would point to the substantially lower average persistence and seriousness of women's offending as compared with that of men, and to the relatively small total number of female offenders. These differences speak not only to the seriousness of female crime but also to the strength of the public demand for women's punishment. Yet in recent years, judgements of desert have increasingly been swayed by popular demand - not only by genuine moral disapproval or fear of crime but also by prejudice, by irresponsible and inaccurate media reporting, by moral panics and unreasoned anxieties.

3.11   Prevailing principles of punishment therefore provide only a limited framework for assessing prison policy in relation to women. Nonetheless, as we have tried to show, even this framework suggests that there should be a reduction in the use of imprisonment for women. That this is so is reflected in the remarkable consensus prevailing in recent public inquiries and reports on the penal system. The Home Affairs Select Committee,[91] the Chief Inspector of Prisons[92] and the Social Work Services and Prisons Inspectorate for Scotland[93] have all argued within the last two years for a radical reduction in women's imprisonment.[94]

A new set of principles

3.12   The case for reduction in the use of imprisonment for women can be made more compelling within the context of a revised set of penal principles -

88   For a general discussion of incapacitation, see Tarling, R. (1993) *Analysing Offending: Data, Models and Interpretation*, London: HMSO.

89   Wolfe, T. (1999), op. cit.

90   Hobcraft, J. (1998), op. cit.

91   Home Affairs Select Committee (1998), *Alternatives to Prison Sentences: Third Report of the Home Affairs Select Committee*, London: HMSO.

92   HM Chief Inspector of Prisons (1997), op. cit.

93   Social Work Services and Prisons Inspectorate for Scotland (1998), op. cit.

94   Our visits to women's prisons further suggest that many prison officers share the Chief Inspector's view that no more than 30 per cent of the present number of women prisoners should in fact be incarcerated.

principles which would draw on the deeper intuitions underpinning the present system, yet which would also relate these intuitions to the values and commitments informing other areas of social policy. In particular, it is time to integrate a principled criminal justice policy with the general commitment to policies which minimise social exclusion.

3.13   We have advanced four main reasons for modifying the desert-based interpretation of the Criminal Justice Act 1991:

- The desert criterion is indeterminate: it fails to establish any concrete guidelines as to the proper measure of punishment.

- In the context of insistent popular anxiety about crime, the desert criterion offers no firm basis for a principled resistance to increased, ineffective severity in punishment. Indeed it sits happily with a political rhetoric which celebrates rather than tempers the retributive emotions and the demand for vengeance.

- This upward drift in levels of punishment - and notably for our purposes in the use of imprisonment - is susceptible to no evaluation or assessment: it is simply presented as justified irrespective of its social costs or consequences.

- Finally, the desert framework has in practice already been diluted by the judicial and legislative introduction of a number of consequentialist principles - principles whose pragmatic and piecemeal adoption has led to an incoherent penal policy.

3.14   We have also commented on the inadequacy of the purely goal-based approach. We now propose the reconstruction of contemporary penal policy around a somewhat different set of principles: principles which are implicit in much contemporary practice, yet whose further articulation might usefully inform future developments.

The rights and responsibilities of citizenship

3.14.1   To reiterate the point with which our discussion began, the criminal justice system should be designed so as to foster respect for the rights and responsibilities of citizenship and to provide for the potential realisation of those rights to the greatest extent compatible with a similar possibility for all other citizens. The reciprocal obligations of citizenship both inform the justification of punishment and set limits to penal practice: crime violates duties of citizenship and hence demands censure, yet society's response to crime must itself be consistent with offenders' status as citizens and must aim to foster social inclusion.

Evaluation by social outcomes

3.14.2   Criminal justice policy should be judged in terms of its social outcomes and these outcomes should be closely monitored and evaluated through research. This is not to imply that the various effects of punishment can simply be measured and traded off against one another. Clearly, some social values - respect for human rights, for example - will generate standards which penal practice must respect. The evaluation principle does imply, however, that social decisions about punishment must always be made in the light of the best evidence about its likely impact.

3.14.3 This principle coheres with the government's commitment to the efficient use of public resources and in particular with the Treasury's recent statement of objectives and the Home Office's commitment to evidence-based criminal justice policy development. Yet it also has an important civil libertarian dimension: the costly state power to punish should only be exercised to the extent that it can reasonably be believed to have beneficial social outcomes.

Coherence in policy making

3.14.4 Criminal justice policy should always be designed with the full range of criminal justice and social policy objectives in mind. This has two dimensions. On the one hand, it implies that practices of punishment must cohere with other practices in the criminal justice system, taking full account of interaction between practices at different stages of the criminal process. Thus, for example, the effect of mandatory sentences in increasing the importance both of discretionary decisions about whether to prosecute and of plea- and charge-bargaining between defendants, prosecutors and courts must always be taken into account. On the other hand, the principle of integration implies that criminal justice policy in general, and penal policy in particular, must also serve broader social goals. This means that, for example, short term gains in crime prevention - whether through deterrence, incapacitation or otherwise - must be balanced against principles of citizenship and objectives such as social inclusion.

Reconciling reprobation, reparation and reintegration

3.14.5 The fundamental rationale of punishment should consist in the objectives of reprobation, reparation and reintegration. Penal policies and penal practices should aim to make these objectives compatible with one another and to reconcile them wherever they conflict.

3.14.6 Reprobation: The adjudication of criminal wrongs is, as a matter of logic, concerned with reprobation; that is penal censure and harsh treatment proportionate to the seriousness of the offence. It is at root concerned to express, through state censure, the community's disapproval of an offender's violation of a key social standard. Reprobation may involve harsh treatment or may take a primarily symbolic form; in this, it differs from the retributive notion of 'an eye for an eye'. However, in common with the key insight of the retributive tradition, penal reprobation is a judgement upon an offence; it does not express a global judgement on the character of the offender.[95] The offender remains at all times a citizen who is entitled to be treated with dignity and to be treated as a

---

[95] Hence, as we argue further in Chapter 4, the Criminal Justice Act 1991's sentencing criterion of 'commensurability with the seriousness of the offence' may be interpreted in reprobative as much as retributive terms; cf. Von Hirsch, A. (1993), op. cit.

responsible subject. The stigmatising and otherwise exclusionary effects of punishment must therefore always be minimised and its reintegrative effects fostered wherever possible.

3.14.7   Reparation: Conversely, the citizenship rights of both victims and the community at large dictate that punishment should, wherever possible, provide an occasion for the offender to make reparation to those affected by the offence.[96] The development of penalties which allow or require offenders to make reparation either directly to their victims or to society as a whole - current examples include the new system of reparation orders for young offenders[97] - are therefore to be preferred to penalties which fracture the social ties and relationships which are needed to underpin any future reintegration.

3.14.8   Reintegration: We want to be clear about the scope and limits of this particular argument. Many crime problems simply cannot be resolved exclusively in terms of criminal justice policy. Without the substantial benefits of citizenship - employment, decent housing, good education - many offenders have an insufficient stake in society to give them adequate incentives to avoid future offending. In this context, penalties such as imprisonment have little effect, and such effect as they have consists in short term incapacitation combined with longer term stigmatisation, which is liable to destroy any chance of reintegration.[98] Yet, in the context of widespread social exclusion, even restorative, deliberately reintegrative penalties have little hope of making a serious impact on rates of reoffending. The scope for genuine reintegration purely through criminal justice is severely circumscribed: the best that can be done is to design penalties so as to limit their disintegrative effects and to provide opportunities, where possible, for social reintegration. This is precisely why criminal justice policy must be integrated with other goals of social policy - with good education, adequate housing, decent welfare safety nets and high levels of employment. Hence current government initiatives such as Sure-Start, Welfare to Work, Education Maintenance Allowances, After-School Clubs and measures to reduce truancy should all be seen as integral to criminal justice policy.

* * * * * * * * * * * * *

3.15   From these basic principles follow three further, more specific, precepts:

Parsimony

3.15.1   It follows from the principle of evaluation by social outcomes that the state's power to punish should be exercised parsimoniously. Some punishment is needed for minimum levels of necessary deterrence and, in special cases, for incapacitation. But the state should inflict the smallest amount of punishment adequate to protect the community from crime.[99]

---

96   On the relationship between reparation and retribution, see Zedner, L. (1994), 'Reparation and Retribution: Are They Reconcilable?', *Modern Law Review* 57, p.228.

97   Crime and Disorder Act 1998 s.67-68.

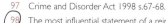

98   The most influential statement of a reintegrative approach to punishment is to be found in the work of Braithwaite, J. (1989), op. cit.; Braithwaite, J. and Pettit, P. (1990), *Not Just Deserts*, Oxford: Clarendon Press; Braithwaite, J. and Daly, K. (1994) 'Masculinities and Communitarian Control' in T. Newburn and E. Stanko, (eds.) *Just Boys Doing Business?* London: Routledge; see also Duff, R.A. (1986), *Trials and Punishments*, Cambridge: Cambridge University Press.

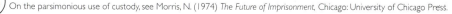

99   On the parsimonious use of custody, see Morris, N. (1974) *The Future of Imprisonment*, Chicago: University of Chicago Press.

Non-discrimination

3.15.2   All practices and principles of punishment should be such as to be capable of being applied in a non-discriminatory way to all citizens irrespective of sex, racial, ethnic, religious, class or other differences.

Accountability

3.15.3   All practices of punishment should be subject to processes of democratic accountability.

From principles to practice

3.16   These new principles and objectives have broad practical implications. For example, the reprobative/reparative as opposed to retributive approach to punishment has important implications for the victims of crime. It is often argued that only retributive punishments take seriously the victim's experience: only by meting out the offender's just deserts can victims feel that 'their' offender has been held properly accountable. Yet, ironically, the sorts of penalties conventionally understood as retributive do little, beyond the symbolic, to address the victim's loss or their feelings of affront, pain and fear.

3.17   Clearly, in the case of very serious offences against the person such as homicide or other grave violence or sexual abuse,[100] the scope for genuine reparation is minimal, and the demands of reprobation - and, in some cases, of incapacitation - indicate a sentence of imprisonment. But in the case of the vast majority of crimes - property crimes, less serious offences against the person, as well as regulatory offences - there may well be scope to work out a package of reparation which could provide some satisfaction for victims. The Thames Valley Police are currently running a pilot on restorative justice which is being evaluated. If this proves to be successful, a system which communicates not only reprobation but also the invitation to reintegrate would be substantially better than one which communicated only retribution or deterrence.

3.18   The principle of parsimony implies the development and application of a rich set of community penalties, incorporating adequate means of tackling drug and alcohol dependence.[101] And it dictates that, in the cases where an incapacitative penalty such as imprisonment is absolutely necessary, the degree of security and control exercised should be strictly proportionate to the degree and quality of risk posed by an individual offender.

3.19   Taken together, the principles of reparation, reintegration and parsimony imply that imprisonment should not be used as a last resort for petty persistent offenders.

---

100   See Hudson, B.A. (1998) 'Restorative Justice: The Challenge of Sexual and Racial Violence', *Journal of Law and Society* 25, p.237.

101   See Morris, N. and Tonry, M. (1990), *Between Prison and Probation: Intermediate Punishments in a Rational Sentencing System* New York: Oxford University Press. In this context, we welcome the introduction of Drug Treatment and Testing Orders under the Crime and Disorder Act 1998 ss. 61-64, albeit with some reservations: see 5.37.

Further, the principle of accountability entails, for example, the regular gathering and publication of data about state punishment, including its financial cost; the development of an adequate - properly funded, independent - Inspectorate monitoring all areas of penal practice; and its investment with sufficient power to ensure that its recommendations are implemented.

The need for responsible public debate

3.20   The proposals in the last section are grounded in intuitions, commitments and values which are widely shared in contemporary Britain. Yet their application in the field of punishment would, in certain respects, be controversial. This is partly because of the strength of the popular demand for severity in punishment; partly also because this demand has been fed over the last two decades by successive governments whose policies have at once asserted the validity of retributive emotions, recognised the reality of the misery caused by crime, and made extravagant promises about government's capacity to reduce it through punishment.

3.21   Perhaps the most important barrier to any move towards a more parsimonious and enlightened penal policy lies in the poor quality of this public debate about crime. As long as governments effectively agree to satisfy the retributive demands of an anxious populace, irrespective of the social consequences of doing so, it will appear as if we, as a society, have no choices in this area. We have simply to punish to the extent of (what is at the particular moment regarded as) desert and the necessary prison places must be provided.

3.22   A responsible government is one which sets real choices before its electorate. And it is one which therefore makes available the facts on the basis of which that electorate can make informed decisions. There is, therefore, a need for honesty and realism on the part of both Government and media: honesty about the real proportion of crime actually processed by the system and realism about the impossibility of 'perfect enforcement'; honesty about the consequences of punishment and realism about its potential to reduce crime. There has already been imaginative thinking about the range of community and financial penalties, and about broader policies to combat social exclusion.[102] But unless the links between social policy and criminal justice policy are made more explicit, and unless the content of community penalties is fully specified, publicised and consistently applied in the context of an informed public debate, they risk being seen merely as a 'soft option'. Then valuable policy initiatives will be unlikely to bear real fruit.

---

102   See above 2.38 – 2.40.

15

4 Equitable Sentencing

4.1   The size of the prison population depends upon a complex set of decisions by politicians, criminal justice professionals, judges, magistrates and indeed citizens about how to respond to offending behaviour. Key among these, and the most public of all of them, is the sentencing decision. In this chapter, we examine the current sentencing framework in England and Wales.

4.2   **Table 4** gives a picture of the way in which the range of penalties available to the courts has been used, distinguishing between their application to men and women and also illustrating the way their use has changed over the last few years.

Table 4

Persons aged 21 and over sentenced for indictable offences by type of sentence or order (percentage)

Year	Total	Discharge	Fine	Probation Order	Community Service Order	Combination Order	Curfew Order	Fully Suspended Sentence	Partly Suspended Sentence	Unsuspended Sentence	Otherwise dealt with	Total immediate custody	Total community sentences
Men													
1991	100	15	39	8	8	*	*	10	1	18	2	18	16
1992	100	17	37	9	9	0	*	8	0	17	3	18	18
1993	100	18	38	10	11	2	*	1	*	18	3	18	23
1994	100	16	36	11	11	2	*	1	*	20	2	20	25
1995	100	15	34	11	11	3	0	1	*	24	2	24	24
1996	100	14	33	11	10	3	0	1	*	26	3	26	24
1997	100	14	32	11	9	3	0	1	*	26	3	26	24
1998	100	14	32	11	9	4	0	1	*	27	3	27	24
Women													
1991	100	34	28	17	4	*	*	8	0	6	2	6	21
1992	100	36	27	16	5	0	*	7	0	6	2	6	21
1993	100	34	31	17	6	1	*	2	*	7	2	7	24
1994	100	32	28	19	7	2	*	2	*	8	2	8	28
1995	100	30	26	20	7	3	–	2	*	10	2	10	30
1996	100	28	25	21	7	3	0	2	*	12	2	12	31
1997	100	27	24	21	7	3	0	2	*	13	2	13	31
1998	100	27	23	21	7	3	0	2	*	14	3	14	31

Source: Home Office Criminal Statistics 1997, Table 7.11. updated by the Home Office

4.3   The most notable features are:

● The use of immediate custody for people aged 21 and over, sentenced for indictable offences has increased for both men and women, but most notably for the latter. Over a quarter of men and 13 per cent of women were sentenced to immediate custody in 1997.[103]

● The use of absolute and conditional discharge declined for women.

● The use of fines for both men and women decreased sharply.

● The use of the suspended sentence for both men and women virtually disappeared following restrictions which required that it should be used only in exceptional circumstances. (Together with the decline in the use of fines, this feature has contributed to the increased use of custody.)

● The use of community sentences for both men and women increased to the point where a quarter of men and just under a third of women received such sentences.

4.4   In the light of the facts about women in prison described in **Chapter 1** and **Chapter 2**, we are particularly disturbed by the increase in the use of custody for women. We would be happy to support more general strategies for the reduction in the use of imprisonment for both men and women; but we realise that, at the present moment, there is neither the political will nor probably public support for Ministers or the judiciary to embark on such a campaign. So at the moment the more pragmatic question is how the current legislative and administrative framework within which sentencing decisions are taken can be made to foster an appropriately parsimonious use of custodial sentences.

4.5   Our argument is therefore not for a radical reform of sentencing or of the penalties available to the courts but rather for:

> *a fresh interpretation of the Criminal Justice Act 1991 in the light of the principles set out in Chapter 3; for a consistent implementation of the legislative framework within adequate structures of accountability; and for an elaboration of the guidance given to sentencing courts on the use of financial and community penalties.*

The current sentencing framework

4.6   Until 1991, the decision about how sentences should be used was relatively little regulated with judges and, to a lesser extent, magistrates enjoying a broad discretion within the generous boundaries set by specific legislative measures and (patchy) guidance from the Court of Appeal. This discretionary

---

103 Home Office (1998), *Criminal Statistics England and Wales 1997*, London: HMSO, table 7.14. The proportionate use of custody for females at all courts for indictable offences reached 13.3 per cent in 1997, continuing the upward trend since 1990 when just over 5 per cent of females were sentenced to immediate custody.

system led to concerns that a suitable balance between the various possible aims of sentencing was not being achieved and that sentencing practice was widely disparate across the country.

The Criminal Justice Act 1991

4.7   The Criminal Justice Act 1991 accordingly established the 'seriousness of the offence' as the principle guideline for determining the severity of the sentence - 'so serious' that only a custodial sentence could be justified, and 'serious enough' to justify a community sentence. The Act therefore imposed a structure on the sentencing process, to which was added a requirement for the court to give reasons for its sentencing decisions.

The main policies underlying the Act - the institution of a consistent and transparent sentencing practice, the parsimonious use of custody, and the principle that the severity of penalties should relate to the offence itself and not to any broader judgement on the offender's character - resonate loudly with the principles defined in the previous chapter.

4.8   In spite of its "parsimonious" intentions, however, the new legislative framework has in fact coincided with a steady increase in the prison population. Two reasons for this development are particularly relevant to the women's prison population:-

● First, the 1991 Act itself expressly excepted from its proportionality principle sentences that might be passed to incapacitate 'dangerous' repeat offenders in the areas of violent and sexual crime. This should in principle have had little impact upon women who (**1.20-1.23**) are less likely than men to commit such crimes. But, in the light of a changing political climate, the incapacitative element of the 1991 Act has subsequently been built upon - most vividly in the Crime (Sentences) Act of 1997, whose extension of mandatory minimum sentences to the area of drug offending has proved to be of major importance for the treatment of women offenders. The Home Secretary's recent announcement of plans for the preventive detention of psychopaths - that is those with dangerous severe personality disorder - constitutes another example of the growing influence of the goal of incapacitation.

● Secondly, the 1991 Act, like all sentencing statutes that stop short of imposing fixed penalties, has proved vulnerable to changes in political climate. The idea of 'commensurability', constrained only by high statutory maximum sentences, dictates no particular sentence, and, during periods in which fear of crime and punitive popular demands are increasing, has proved to be an ineffective tool in enforcing parsimonious sentencing practice. On the contrary, one could argue that the rhetoric of 'desert' becomes, under some conditions, a further impetus for increased severity, while also justifying that severity without reference to its consequences.

4.9   We would argue that a situation in which any costly social policy such as imprisonment is impervious to measurement or evaluation is inconsistent with the Treasury's recent statement of objectives for the development and assessment of public policy across Departments. It also sits uneasily with the Home Office's decision to devote substantial resources to the evaluation of crime reduction strategies in pursuit of a rigorous, evidence-based approach to criminal justice practice.

4.10   The indeterminacy of the 1991 Act is further illustrated by the ease with which the principle of commensurability was diluted by judicial interpretation of the legislative provisions. For example, soon after its implementation, judicial interpretation held that the prevalence of a particular offence might be taken as aggravating the gravity of a specific instance of that offence - hence allowing the goal of deterrence in through the back door.[104]

4.11   Another illustration of the dilution of the 1991 Act's principled stance was the speed with which the judiciary and magistracy were able to undermine the Act's provisions on previous convictions. Originally, an offender's criminal record was meant to be relevant only if it affected the gravity of the present offence, reflecting the idea that the penalty should be commensurate merely with the current offence. However, sentencers were able to take the sting out of the provision by interpreting record as cancelling mitigation.[105] As early as 1993, sentencers' vociferous protests against what they nonetheless saw as an assault on the independence of the sentencing function resulted in amending legislation which restored their unrestricted right to take previous convictions into account. More recent legislation such as the Crime (Sentences) Act 1997 and the Crime and Disorder Act 1998 have further underlined the importance of deterrence as an aim of sentencing.

The focus on law and order 1992 - 1997

4.12   From 1992 until the General Election of 1997, there was a political focus on 'law and order' which was more acute even than that which characterised the early years of the Thatcher administration. This was an era in which 'prison works' became an axiom rather than a reasoned political claim based upon empirical evidence. The present Government may, however, be less dogmatic and its emphasis on the efficient use of public resources an important impetus to the development of mechanisms for evaluating the effects of penal policies.

4.13   Yet the ramifications of the focus on law and order are still being felt, both in the Government's insistence that it is appropriate to be 'tough on crime' and in the continuing effects of a range of judicial and legislative decisions made during the previous administration.

4.14   In particular, three factors are still highly influential. In the first place, there subsists a strong belief in the deterrent effect of imprisonment - a belief

---

104   Cunningham (1993) 96 Criminal Appeal Reports, 422.

105   Bexley (1993) 14 Criminal Appeal Reports, 462

apparently impervious to empirical evidence which shows that, while the criminal justice system as a whole is capable of having deterrent effects, marginal changes in the severity of punishment have little impact on its deterrent effect.[106] Secondly, a certain scepticism about the penal adequacy of community penalties appears to have survived the fall of the last administration, notwithstanding some positive developments in the fields of restorative justice and the implementation of new community penalties. Finally, in the full implementation of the mandatory sentence policy embodied in the Crime (Sentences) Act 1997, we have a sentencing provision based on a mix of political opportunism, retributive rhetoric, and appeals to incapacitative and deterrent effects unsupported by evidence.

The Sentencing Advisory Panel

4.15   Notwithstanding the indeterminacy of the 1991 Act, however, we would argue that the best hope for a rational sentencing process lies in a return to its framework, interpreted in the light of the goals of reprobation, reparation and reintegration which we have posited in **Chapter 3** and which are not only consistent with the principles informing the Act but also find expression in several significant developments since 1997. Moreover, we believe that the recent appointment of a Sentencing Advisory Panel under the Crime and Disorder Act provides an opportunity for a fresh interpretation of the 1991 Act, building upon its central ideas and clarifying its relationship to subsequent legislation. We make a number of recommendations for expanding the work of the Panel which may call for an amendment of the Panel's statutory basis in Section 80-81 of the Crime and Disorder Act 1998.[107]

Implications for sentencing

4.16   If the current legislative and administrative framework within which sentencing decisions are made is, in future, to foster the use of appropriately parsimonious sentences for women, then we believe there are three implications for sentencing.

4.17   First, efficiency and genuine equity in sentencing can only be achieved if sentencers concern themselves with the impact of the sentences which they impose on all concerned including dependants.[108] This requires that:

> **The distinctive position of women offenders and, in particular, of the large numbers of women with primary responsibility for small children, should be taken into account as one factor relevant to the determination of sentence.**

4.18   Examples of factors relevant to the determination of sentence include

---

106   Von Hirsch, A., Bottoms, A., Burney, E. and Wikstrom, P.O. (1999), *Criminal Deterrence and Sentencing Severity: An Analysis of Recent Research*, Oxford: Hart Publishing. .

107   The role of the Sentencing Advisory Panel is "*to provide views to the Court of Appeal to help the Court in framing sentencing guidelines. The guidelines of the Court of Appeal are a part of case law and the lower courts must follow them when passing sentence. When the Court of Appeal plans to make guidelines on an offence or a particular group of offences, it will alert the Panel and the Panel will provide views. The Panel will also provide views when it feels the need to do so itself and when the Home Secretary directs it to do so. The Panel will meet regularly to prepare its views. Whenever it is preparing its views on an offence group or offences, it will consult a number of organisations which the Lord Chancellor has nominated for this purpose. When providing its views to the Court of Appeal, the Panel will also pass on information about what sentences have been imposed for the relevant offences in recent years and about how expensive or effective the available sentences are.*" Home Office (1999), Sentencing Advisory Panel – Background. Factsheet 1, London: Home Office.

108   See Ashworth, A. and Player, E. (1998), 'Sentencing, Equal Treatment, and the Impact of Sanctions' and Hudson. B. 'Doing Justice to Difference', both in A. Ashworth and M. Wasik (eds.), *Fundamentals of Sentencing Theory* Oxford: Oxford University Press p.251 and 223.

the weight of significance to be attached to childhood or recent experiences of physical or sexual abuse; the offender's economic position; the offender's relationships with, and responsibilities towards, children, partners, parents or other family or household members; and the effect on such people of any sentence which the court may have in mind.[109] The evidence presented in **Chapter 1** argues particularly for the need to take account of a history of mental ill health. There is copious anecdotal evidence within the Prison Service, furthermore, that custody has an especially devastating effect upon women. If research could validate this professional judgement, it would be both equitable and consistent with the principle of evaluating penalties by their likely consequences for sentencers to take this into account in deciding sentence. Furthermore, these factors may in certain circumstances raise questions of mitigation.

> *We would urge the Court of Appeal and the Sentencing Advisory Panel to give immediate attention to mitigating factors which may be of particular significance to women.*

4.19   This is not, it should be emphasised, a case of special pleading for women but a principle which should be applied across the board. If it were, it would be consistent with long-established anti-discrimination norms, which prohibit not only direct, prejudiced discrimination but the discrimination which occurs indirectly when apparently neutral criteria have an unjustifiably unequal impact upon members of different sexes or ethnic groups.[110] Equality requires all groups to have an equal chance of relevant provision. It is a principle which in the criminal justice context received official recognition in the institution of the unit fine system in 1991. It is, in our view, a matter of deep regret that the enlightened experiment of unit fines was of such short duration.

> *We recommend that the Government, with advice from the Sentencing Advisory Panel, should consider whether a form of 'unit fine' might be reintroduced, perhaps on a non-statutory basis, as a means of deciding – and explaining publicly – the amount of the fine which would be proportionate in the circumstances of a particular offence and offender.*

4.20   Secondly, the principle of equity thus requires that the information available to sentencers on which they base their decisions should be adequate for them to do so. Yet there is evidence that the kinds of information available to sentencers via pre-sentence reports vary in significant respects for men and women and according to ethnic group.[111] We support the use of pre-sentence reports

109   See Hudson, B. (1998), 'Mitigation for Socially Deprived Offenders', in A. Ashworth and A. Von Hirsch (eds.), *Principled Sentencing* Oxford: Hart Publishing, p.205.

110   Sex Discrimination Act 1975 s.1(1)(b); Race Relations Act 1976, s.1(1)(b).

111   See Social Work and Prisons Inspectorates for Scotland (1998) op. cit. Chapter 2; Hedderman, C. and Gelsthorpe, L. (1997), (eds.) op. cit.; Farrington, D. and Morris, A. (1989), op.cit.; Eaton, M. (1986) *Justice for Women*, Oxford: Oxford University Press; see also Allen, H. (1987), *Justice Unbalanced*, Oxford: Oxford University Press - a study which demonstrated courts' willingness to accept and solicit evidence of mental disorder as a factor in female offending - and their corresponding reluctance to accept such evidence in relation to men.

and would like to see properly funded research on the quality and consistency of such reports and in particular on their relative use for men and women.

> **We believe that the courts should always call for, and carefully consider, a pre-sentence report in any case involving a woman offender where a custodial or community sentence may be in prospect.**

4.21   Moreover, if factors such as family responsibilities, mental illness, and educational standing are relevant to the sentencing of women, they are equally relevant to the sentencing of men. We believe that practice in this area could and should be improved by the refinement of guidelines available to both courts and those writing the reports.

4.22   We also believe it could be improved by training. Sentencers should be aware of the existing research on female offending and the impact of penalties on women offenders. They should also be thoroughly familiar with the special problems and characteristics of the female prison estate which result in the distinctively punitive features of imprisonment for women (**Chapter 2**).

4.23   Thirdly, it is important that courts do not too quickly or easily assume that certain penalties are unsuitable for women because of their financial position or their domestic responsibilities. Indeed, there is research evidence to suggest that substantial numbers of magistrates are reluctant to impose fines upon many women offenders.[112] The view that penalties such as community service are unsuitable for those with significant childcare responsibilities may well be inhibiting the use of otherwise appropriate penalties; this may also become relevant to the use of Drug Treatment and Testing Orders. Conversely, there is a risk that Home Detention Curfew may be less available to women given that a higher proportion of women than of men prisoners lose their home during their period in custody.[113] This effective sidelining of certain penalties for women entails that women experience a 'shorter tariff' then men; in other words, the journey up the ladder of penal severity towards a custodial sentence may be shorter for them.[114] Without adequate guidance on their use, the addition of new community penalties will not necessarily lengthen that journey or reduce the use of custody by the sentencers of women.

The need for guidelines

4.24   Hence we believe that both the elaboration of sentencing guidelines for the use of community penalties and the practical modification of some of those penalties[115] would bring about greater fairness and more justice in both the sentencing and treatment of women offenders.[116] It would in the process reduce the numbers of women being sentenced to custody.

---

112   See Hedderman, C. and Gelsthorpe, L. (1997), op. cit. For further discussion of evidence on the sexually differentiated use of non-custodial penalties, see 5.23 – 5.29.

113   See further 5.46 – 5.48; and Wolfe, T. (1999) op. cit. It is rather early to judge the operation of H.D.C. We were told by the Home Office that before it was introduced it was estimated that there would be 3,740 males and 260 females on curfew when it was fully implemented. In July 1999, however, only 48 per cent of expected males compared with 78 per cent of expected females were actually on H.D.C.

114   See Moxon, D. (1989), *Sentencing Practice in the Crown Courts*, Home Office Research Study 103, London: Home Office; evidence from the US suggests that similar factors affect the sentencing of members of ethnic minority groups: see Daly, K. and Tonry, M. (1997), 'Gender, Race and Sentencing' in M. Tonry, (ed.) *Crime and Justice: A Review of Research*, 22, 201.

115   See 5.37 – 5.49.

116   Morris, N. and Tonry, M. (1990), *Between Prison and Probation: Intermediate Punishments in a Rational Sentencing System* New York: Oxford University Press.

4.25   The elaboration of relevant sentencing guidelines is of particular importance given that the current system of guideline judgements issued by the Court of Appeal is overwhelmingly concerned with custodial sentencing in the context of serious offences against the person. The consistent use of the wide range of community penalties is crucial to their credibility with the general public, particularly in the context of continuing evidence of wide regional variations in sentencing practice.[117] We therefore see the elaboration of guidelines for the use of financial and community penalties in fields such as property crime, minor offences against the person and drug offences by the Court of Appeal, the Sentencing Advisory Panel and in the Magistrates' Association's sentencing guidelines, as having a potentially decisive role to play in the constructive implementation of community penalties across the board.

A fresh interpretation of The Criminal Justice Act 1991

4.26   We regard the institution of the Sentencing Advisory Panel (1997) as providing a real opportunity for a clear restatement of the principles underlying the 1991 Act. However, we note with regret the limited terms in which the Panel's statutory responsibilities are framed and hope that these will be expanded and/or amended so as to allow the Panel to develop the strategic role envisaged in our recommendations.[118] The need to strike a balance between the demands of reprobation, reintegration and reparation means that, on occasion, censure and the opportunity to make amends through various forms of restorative justice, rather than penal harsh treatment, may be an appropriate sentence. There will also be occasions for mercy and compassion, even if these words are nowadays rarely used.[119] We welcome in this respect the piloting of reprimands and warnings and of reparation and action plan orders for young offenders under the Crime and Disorder Act 1998.

> *The piloting of reprimands and warnings (and of reparation and action plan orders) is a development which we hope will be extended to adult offenders in the future. We suggest that women offenders would provide an eminently suitable group for further pilot studies.*

4.27   Consistent with the principle of parsimony, the seriousness of the offence should therefore be treated as setting the upper limit for the loss or curtailment of liberty (or amount of the fine) to be imposed, not as providing a norm to which punishment should always be attached. If, exceptionally, the limit has to be exceeded for public protection, the justification should be rigorously tested in court and the court's decision should be fully explained. Where the outcome is a disproportionate period in custody, special restrictions on movement, or a

---

117   See for example Prison Reform Trust (1997), *Sentencing: A Geographical Lottery*. London: Prison Reform Trust.

118   Section 81 of the Crime and Disorder Act refers to the Panel proposing guidelines "for a particular category of offence". If interpreted narrowly, this would hamper the Panel's ability to develop guidelines in more general matters such as the mitigating factors of special relevance to women.

119   In this context, Judges and Ministers might usefully ponder the dialogue between Isabella and Angelo in Act II, Scene ii of Shakespeare's *Measure for Measure*.

prolonged or intrusive form of surveillance, those restrictions should not be regarded as punishment and should be subject to special conditions, safeguards and mechanisms for review.

Transparency

4.28   Of particular importance to women is the implication of the principles of parsimony and reintegration that, wherever loss or curtailment of liberty has to be imposed, the sentence should allow the offender the greatest possible opportunity to retain, restore or establish links with her family and with the community more widely. She should be enabled, and expected, to exercise her rights and responsibilities as a citizen, and to make some form of reparation where that is practicable, either to the victim or to the wider community. The court should decide and make clear any requirements or conditions which would attract sanctions for failure to comply, and should be informed of any programmes of education, training or treatment in which the offender would take part under the terms of a court order. Courts should not be expected to decide, approve or supervise those programmes, which involve professional rather than judicial skills and judgement. But:

> **Courts should be entitled, and encouraged, to make a report to the Home Office if they consider the facilities made available to an offender to be inadequate; and to call for accounts of an offender's progress, with the possibility of a similar report to the Home Office if they consider her progress to have been prejudiced by the poor standard of the facilities provided. The offender should herself be given an opportunity to contribute to that account.**

4.29   We attach particular importance to the issue of accountability for sentencing decisions which should be open, intelligible and arrived at through a process which is seen as fair and consistent. These considerations should apply to the use of community penalties and should if necessary form grounds for appeal. They should help the sentence to be better understood not only by the offender and her family but also by the victim and by the media and broader community.

We therefore strongly support a structured, step by step approach to sentencing in which the court has to consider, in sequence, the nature of the offence, including the effect on any victim, aggravating or mitigating factors, and the circumstances of the offender, before coming to a view on the sentence. A structured approach based on accurate information guards against discrimination or prejudice, and enables reasons to be formulated which can be explained in open court.

We would also welcome a restatement by the Court of Appeal, with advice from the Sentencing Advisory Panel, of the principles upon which sentencing should proceed, re-emphasising the need for sentencing to be rational, consistent and transparent, acknowledging that the cost of the sentence is a relevant consideration for the sentencing court (as it is by statute for the Sentencing Advisory Panel).

In accordance with these principles, we would oppose any minimum limit on the sentences available to the court. Our one recommendation for legislation on sentencing is therefore to urge the immediate repeal of Part I of the Crime (Sentences) Act 1997.

Sentencing practice should be more closely monitored following these changes.

Joined-up policy in the field of sentencing

4.30   Sentencing is a prime example of an issue where policies cry out to be joined up. Its ramifications extend throughout the criminal justice system and beyond it to the fields of social services, health, housing, education and employment - not only for offenders themselves, but also for their households and dependants. Yet the Government has chosen to distance itself from any consideration of the social and economic implications of sentencing. It has done so on the grounds that sentencing is 'entirely a matter for the courts'. Yet it has not only left in place those provisions of the Crime (Sentences) Act which had already been approved when it came into office but has extended them to include mandatory minimum sentences of imprisonment for repeated offences of burglary. The Government claims to have made provision for the extra prison places which mandatory minimum sentences will demand. But it has never acknowledged the effect which such decisions, and its political stance as a whole, can have on sentencing practice more generally. Its policy on prison accommodation is in effect based on the principle of 'predict and provide' which has been discredited in all other areas of public expenditure.

4.31   We accept the fundamental principle that the sentence to be imposed in particular cases is a matter of judicial rather than political judgement and that it is therefore for the courts alone. But we regret the fact that this principle has sometimes been distorted to justify the Government's withdrawal from its proper responsibility for promoting legislation and establishing administrative procedures through which sentencing principles can be established and practice can be developed and reviewed. The report of Lord Woolf's Inquiry into the prison disturbances in April 1990 shows that the members of the Inquiry recognised this point. [120] They addressed it in their proposal for the formation of a national Criminal Justice Consultative Council and area criminal justice committees. The government of the day accepted their proposals, and the Council and area committees are still in existence. Yet they have never developed the strategic role that Lord Woolf's Inquiry intended. We believe that the development of this strategic role, along with better co-ordination between sentencers and the Criminal Justice Consultative Council and area committees, might improve the general quality of sentencing decisions and in particular, by building up local co-ordination, might foster the regional consistency of sentencing.

> **The Criminal Justice Consultative Council should be integrated with the Government's own machinery for strategic planning and 'joined-up policy' across the criminal justice system.**

* * * * * * * * * * * * *

4.32   To summarise, we believe that the basic framework of sentencing set out in the Criminal Justice Act 1991 could, with the elaboration of further guidelines by the Court of Appeal, Sentencing Advisory Panel and Magistrates' Association, provide a basis for sentencing women consistently with the principles elaborated and defended in **Chapter 3**.

---

120   Woolf, H. and Tumim, S. (1991), *Prison Disturbances April 1990*, Cm 1456, London: HMSO.

5 Criminal Justice Without Custody

5.1   An effective criminal justice system must protect the public from serious offenders, compensate victims, work to reduce levels of offending, provide for adequate punishment that is commensurate with the seriousness of the offence and for the reintegration of the offender, while using resources efficiently.

5.2   In the last chapter we discussed the principles that we believe should inform sentencing decisions and emphasised the need for parsimony in the use of custody. But if we are to endorse the view that there are too many women in prison and that the present organisation of women's prisons is inappropriate to their needs, then there is an obligation on us to suggest how the criminal justice system should provide for them. How it should provide, that is, for women who offend, for whom prison and the present organisation of women's prisons is inappropriate but who, after the application of the principles advocated in **Chapter 3**, still merit some punishment.

5.3   Clearly, less reliance on custodial sentences presupposes greater use of penalties within the community. Over the last decade there has been considerable expansion in the range of community sentences and the courts have been granted greater flexibility in tailoring penalties to fit the needs of individual offenders. In this chapter we examine the range of non-custodial measures already available and consider their potential for replacing the use of imprisonment for women.

Can we reduce the numbers remanded in custody?

5.4   Before we do this, however, we must consider first the position of that important group of women who are remanded in custody, two-thirds of whom have been neither tried nor sentenced. We saw (**1.11-1.12**) that the numbers of women remanded in custody have been increasing, that they made up a quarter of the female prison population, and yet only 30 per cent eventually receive a custodial sentence.[121] Considering the distress and disruption caused by imprisonment for the women and the difficulties which this creates for the management of prison regimes, this would appear to be an obvious first place to seek a reduction in the female prison population. Yet we know all too little about how and why courts use remand.

5.5   The Bail Act 1976 is based on a presumption in favour of bail, which should only be refused if the court has grounds to believe that the defendant will fail to turn up to trial, that she will offend while on bail, that she will interfere with

---

121   Home Office (1999) *Women and the Criminal Justice System, a section 95 publication*. London: Home Office: London.

witnesses or otherwise obstruct the course of justice, or that custody is necessary for her own protection. We have no data on the relative importance of these different grounds for refusing bail for the women held in prison on remand (except that the risk of a female defendant interfering with witnesses appears to be given a low rating by the courts). But we have noted the Law Commission's recommendation that important parts of the Bail Act should be reviewed to take account of the passage of the Human Rights Act.[122]

> **We recommend that there should be a systematic exploration of bail decisions with a view to reducing the use of custodial remand.**

5.6   Remanding a defendant in custody on the ground that she is likely to offend whilst on bail is only justified if there is a serious risk of grave harm. In reaching their decision the court should take account of the seriousness of the present offence and be guided by two criteria, whether the current offence, if proven, shows convincing evidence that the defendant is capable of causing serious harm to the public, and whether the present offence is sufficiently serious to justify a custodial penalty on retributive grounds. As the data in **Chapter I** show, most of the women on remand in prison have not been charged with offences of such seriousness.

5.7   As for the risk of failing to appear for trial, there are already interesting experiments with bail supervision schemes to reduce that risk by helping the defendant to find accommodation or by providing additional supervision through the remand period. These experiments could be extended. In those cases where the possibility of non-attendance is related to drug dependence or mental disorder, hostel places such as those provided in Crowley House outside Birmingham by the West Midlands Probation Service offer a more constructive setting for awaiting sentence, particularly if, as at Crowley House, the women can be accommodated together with their children.[123] Policies of this kind would reinforce the need for improvements in the quality and availability of pre-sentence reports (**4.20**) and might even lead to diversion from the trial process altogether.

Can we divert more from the prosecution and trial process?

5.8   In the previous chapter, we noted that the sentencing decision was one among a number of stages at which official decision-making determines the ultimate shape and size of the prison population. Before we arrive at the sentence, however, there are a number of formal and informal 'gatekeeping' stages with equally important effects: ordinary citizens' decisions about reporting crime,

---

122   Law Commission (1999), *Bail and the Human Rights Act 1998*, Consultation Paper 157. London: Law Commission.

123   The Committee visited Crowley House probation hostel.

police decisions about recording, investigating and responding to alleged offences, and decisions by the Crown Prosecution Service about whether and at what level to continue the prosecution of alleged offenders. Of particular significance for this report are official agencies' decisions to divert an offender or suspected offender from the prosecution and trial process through the use of the power to issue a formal caution and through the operation of court diversion schemes.

Cautioning

5.9   Over the last two decades, the power of the police not only to give informal warnings but also to issue official cautions has become a key aspect of the administration of justice. Where a person admits their guilt, where there is sufficient evidence to prosecute, and where the person gives their informed consent, the police may decide to record a formal caution rather than proceed through the Crown Prosecution Service. Statistics demonstrate the significance of cautioning for women charged with indictable offences. In 1997, the figures show an overall cautioning rate of 52 per cent for females and of 35 per cent for males.[124]

5.10   As the use of formal cautions has grown, so have concerns about the consistency and fairness of their use. This has resulted in the development of National Standards for cautioning. The most recent of these formal statements, which was issued by the Home Office in 1984,[125] lays down a presumption in favour of not prosecuting certain categories of offender. These categories include the elderly and those who suffer from some serious form of physical illness or mental impairment or illness. This latest Home Office statement also responds to the concern that repeat cautioning was being over-used. The general criteria for decisions to caution - the seriousness of the offence and likely penalty if convicted, the offender's previous record, the offender's attitude to the offence, and the offender's age and state of health - are fleshed out in more detail by guidelines published by the Association of Chief Police Officers in 1998.

5.11   We support the use of cautioning for women offenders, which is consistent with the principle of parsimony. Given the social background of many women offenders, and given the principle that punishment should be equitable in its impact, we would suggest that the demands of reprobation and proportionality will often be satisfied by cautioning. This will be especially so for first offenders, for those who have committed offences of relatively low seriousness, and for the considerable number of women offenders who suffer from mental disorders.

5.12   We would, however, also suggest that improvements could and should be made to the system of cautioning:

● Further steps might be taken to ensure that cautioning is used in a fair and even-handed manner. Cautioning involves a wide measure of police

---

124   Ashworth, A. (1998), *The Criminal Process: An Evaluative Study* (2nd ed.) Oxford: Oxford University Press.
125   Home Office, Police and Criminal Evidence Act 1984, Codes of Practice (3rd. Ed. 1995) Code D.

discretion and there is always the risk that that discretion will be exercised more favourably towards some - perhaps the more socially advantaged - groups of offenders. The risk, particularly with 'caution-plus' schemes which aim to compensate victims (see below), that poorer offenders may be less likely to be selected for a caution is of acute relevance to women. There is evidence that African-Caribbean people are less likely to be cautioned than are either Asian or white people.[126]

● Cautions should wherever possible incorporate an element of restorative justice, which links with our concern with reparation. It is wrong in principle that the decision to caution rather than prosecute an offender should deprive the victim of the opportunity of some reparation. Furthermore, the incorporation of a reparative element would answer the objection that cautions are merely a 'let-off' for the offender. In this respect, we would follow the lead provided by a number of 'caution plus' projects around the country - schemes which combine a caution with reference to a restorative justice or mediation scheme.[127] This would also be consistent with the Crime and Disorder Act's provision for reprimands, warnings and reparation orders for young offenders.

We recommend an increase in the use of cautions for women who have committed offences of low seriousness and particularly for those offenders who are suffering from mental health problems.

Steps should also be taken to ensure that cautions are used more systematically.

Court diversion schemes

5.13   Ultimately, however, a significant number of offenders who might appropriately have been diverted are nonetheless prosecuted and end up in court.

So we attach great importance to the development of court diversion schemes for mentally disordered offenders and women with drug problems.

Again recurrent concerns include the consistency with which such schemes operate around the country and the quality of information - particularly medical information - available to the courts. Concerns also exist as to whether the consequences of diversion are always proportionate to the nature of the

---

126 See Jefferson, T. and Walker, M. (1992), 'Ethnic Minorities in the Criminal Justice System', *Criminal Law Review* p.83 and 88; for possible explanations see Fitzgerald, M. (1993), *Ethnic Minorities and the Criminal Justice System*, Royal Commission on Criminal Justice Research Study 20, p.18, London: HMSO.

127 Some 'caution-plus' schemes provide, additionally or alternatively, for reference to a variety of social interventions such as participation in programmes tackling drug or alcohol abuse. We would also support these schemes, albeit with the proviso that such intervention should always be proportionate to the seriousness of the behaviour to which the offender has admitted: diversion from prosecution should not become an occasion for widening the net of social control.

mentally ill person's offending behaviour - highlighting, ironically, the possibility that offenders may enjoy greater safeguards if actually prosecuted.[128] This area, in our view, merits both more extensive, gender-differentiated research and further practical development.

The range of non-custodial penalties

5.14   The range of non-custodial sentences available to the courts, and particularly the diversity of community penalties, is unsurpassed in any other jurisdiction. Their relative importance and the way that their use for both men and women has changed over the last ten years was summarised in **Table 4** in the last chapter. A brief description of the content of the penalties is provided below in **Table 5**.

Table 5
Summary of Available Non-Custodial Penalties

Self regulatory disposals	Absolute /conditional discharge	Either no further action is taken (absolute), or this may be dependent on future good behaviour.
	Binding Over	An offender will enter a recognizance for a stipulated sum and will be bound over to keep the peace for a certain period of time
Financial	Fines	The most common form of disposal used by the courts.
	Compensation Order	Offenders may be ordered to make financial compensation to the victim of their crime; usually in conjunction with another penalty.
	Confiscation Order	Confiscation of financial assets accrued as a result of criminal activity – often drug trafficking.
Community Penalties	Probation Order	Most common community penalty. Available for offenders aged 16+. The court may add additional requirements such as treatment for drug addiction or mental health problems; attendance at a day centre or residence in a hostel. National Standards were introduced in 1992. New standards come into force on 1 April 2000.
	Community Service Order	Requires an offender aged 16+ to carry out work in the community for between 40 – 240 hours.
	Combination Order	Enables the courts to impose an order on an offender aged 16+ which comprises elements of probation supervision and of unpaid work. Probation may last between 12 months and 3 years. Community Service may be for 40 – 100 hours.
	Curfew Orders	Requires an offender to be in a specified place for 2 – 12 hours a day for a period up to 6 months. They are monitored electronically via a 'tag'.
	Supervision Order	Similar to a Probation Order, but available only for juvenile offenders aged 10 – 17 years. Supervision may be provided either by a Probation Officer or Social Worker. The order may include a residence requirement, and may require the offender to make reparation to their victim. (Not yet generally available)
	Attendance Centre Order	Used only for young offenders, convicted of an imprisonable offence who are in breach of their Probation Order. Offender is required to attend a centre for up to three hours on any one day. The number of hours specified is usually 12, but may be up to 36.
New Orders – Crime and Disorder Act.	Drug Treatment and Testing Order	Allows the court to require an offender to undergo treatment for their drug problem and to be regularly tested. The order requires the offender's consent, and may last between six months and three years. To be implemented in England and Wales in 2000, subject to Ministerial decisions following evaluation of pilots.
	Reparation Order	Requires a young offender to make reparation to their victim or the community. The reparation must not exceed a total of 24 hours, and should be appropriate to the offence.
	Action Plan Order	Tailored to address causes of a child or young person's offending. Requires young offender to comply with three month action plan, supervised by a Probation Officer, Social Worker or member of local Youth Offending Team. Imposes conditions regarding behaviour and whereabouts. (Not yet fully in operation)

128   See Carson, D. (1989), 'Prosecuting People with Mental Handicaps', *Criminal Law Review*, p.87; Burney, E. and Pearson, G. (1995), 'Mentally Disordered Offenders: Finding a Focus for Diversion', *Howard Journal of Criminal Justice*, 34; Peay, J. (1997), 'Mentally Disordered Offenders' in M. Maguire, R. Morgan and R. Reiner (eds.), *Oxford Handbook of Criminology*, Oxford: Clarendon Press, pp.673-674.

5.15   We are not proposing the introduction of new orders. But:

> **We recommend that there should be greater use of these existing provisions and that community penalties should be refocused so as to make them more relevant to women offenders.**

The Criminal Justice Act 1991: in principle

5.16   The Act reconceptualised non-custodial sentences as 'punishment in the community', rather than 'alternatives to custody'. This gave these sentences an independent identity rather than defining them in relation to imprisonment. The legislation made clear that an offender should not be sentenced to custody unless the offence was so serious that only a custodial sentence could be justified.[129] Seen from this perspective, there could be no alternatives to imprisonment.

5.17   In the 1990 White Paper the Government set out its aim to reduce the use of custody and to endorse punishment in the community:

> *"The Government believes a new approach is needed if the use of custody is to be reduced. Punishment in the community should be an effective way of dealing with many offenders, particularly those convicted of property crimes and less serious offences of violence, when financial penalties are insufficient."*[130]

Emphasis was placed on the ways in which community penalties restricted the liberty of offenders and imposed on them a demanding and tough regime.

> *"The punishment should be in the restrictions on liberty and in the enforcement of the orders. All community service orders place restrictions on an offender's liberty, and so may probation orders when, for example, they require an offender to attend a day centre for a lengthy period."*[131]

5.18   The legislation also clarified the hierarchy of sentence severity with discharges at the bottom, followed by financial penalties, community penalties and ultimately imprisonment. Section 6(1) states that a court shall not impose a community sentence unless the offence was 'serious enough' to warrant such a sentence. It was clearly Parliament's intention, therefore, that community penalties should not be given for minor offences. Further more Section 6 (2)(b) makes clear that restrictions on liberty must be commensurate with the seriousness of the offence.

5.19   At the same time the legislation also recognised that community penalties

129 Criminal Justice Act 1991 s. 1 (2) (a).
130 Home Office (1990), *Crime, Justice and Protecting the Public*, London: HMSO para. 4.3.
131 Ibid.

should meet the needs of the offender and provide an element of rehabilitation within the framework of commensurability:

> **"The idea behind this was that the court should consider which of the orders of roughly the same severity (perhaps probation with conditions or community service, or curfew or short community service) might meet the needs of the offender, as outlined in the pre-sentence report."**[132]

Thus legislation provided the courts with greater flexibility in the ways in which they could combine orders and attach requirements in order to tailor sentences to fit individual offenders.

The Criminal Justice Act 1991: in practice

5.20   In **Chapter 4** we showed how the 1991 Act had failed in its aim to reduce the courts' use of custodial penalties. However, **Table 4** in **Chapter 4** also showed that the Government's attempt to encourage sentencers to make greater use of community penalties was not entirely in vain: over a five year period (1992 – 1996) they increased from 20 per cent to 31 per cent of all sentences imposed on women and from 18 per cent to 26 per cent of those on men. But rather than displacing custodial sentences it appears that the courts shifted their sentences up-tariff, using discharges and fines less frequently than before and resorting to tougher community penalties and imprisonment. Professor George Mair's presentation to this Inquiry demonstrated that probation, community service and the combination order were all being used more frequently for less serious offences. Between 1991 and 1997 community penalties were increasingly being imposed on offenders convicted of summary offences:

> **"In 1991, a total of 47,500 offenders were sentenced to a probation order. Almost three-quarters of these were for indictable offences (72 per cent); by 1997 the total was 54,100, of which only two-thirds (66 per cent) were for indictable offences...**

> **For community service the picture is similar. In 1991 there were a total of 42,500 Community Service Orders and 69 per cent of these were for indictable offences; in 1997 the total was 47,100 of which 61 per cent were for indictable offences...**

---

132   Ashworth, A. (1995), *Sentencing and Criminal Justice* (2nd ed.) London: Butterworths, p.254.

"The combination order is the same: in 1993 (the first full year of its operation) there were a total of 8,900, of which 69 per cent were for offenders sentenced for indictable offences; by 1997... there were 19,500 combination orders, of which 60 per cent were for indictable offences... And this is for an order which is seen as being rigorous and demanding for offenders."[133]

5.21   The tougher approach to offenders is confirmed by two further trends in sentencing practice. First, the greater willingness of the courts to attach requirements to probation orders - in 1987 eight out of ten probation orders had no added requirements but by 1997 the proportion had decreased to 67 per cent. Secondly, the tendency for the courts to impose a community penalty on first offenders and those with a limited criminal history. In 1991 one in three offenders starting a community service order (CSO) had previously served a custodial sentence but by 1997 the proportion had dropped to 1 in 5. Conversely, 14 per cent of offenders starting CSOs in 1991 had no previous convictions but by 1997 this had more than doubled to 34 per cent. Similar patterns are evident for probation and combination orders.

Non-custodial penalties for women

5.22   There are, however, important distinctions in the way the courts use the various options for the disposal of male and female offenders. **Table 4** shows that women are significantly more likely than men to receive an absolute or conditional discharge and are more likely to be made the subject of a probation order. They are, however, less likely than men to be fined or given a community service order.

Differential tariffs

5.23   We noted in the previous chapter the research evidence that magistrates actively avoid financial penalties for substantial numbers of women and how this results in some of them being 'down-tariffed' to a discharge and others 'up-tariffed' to a community penalty, usually a probation order.[134] The displacement of financial penalties by community sentences can be particularly problematic if a woman is convicted of further offences, as the courts may impose a more severe penalty and thereby shorten her sentence career and accelerate her progress towards imprisonment. For both men and women the suspended sentence has virtually disappeared.

5.24   The ways in which the courts have both used, and failed to use, CSOs when sentencing women has arguably contributed to the rise in female imprisonment. Although the courts have gradually increased their use of CSOs for women, they represented only 7 per cent of all sentences imposed on

133   Mair, G. (1999), *Community Penalties and Female Offenders*, Paper presented to Committee Seminar on 9 February 1999.

134   Hedderman, C. and Gelsthorpe, L. (1997), op cit.

women in 1997 for indictable offences. It has been suggested that the reluctance of the courts to use this penalty for women has been influenced by its characterisation as a punishment specifically designed for 'fit young men'[135] Recent research by the Howard League suggests that this disinclination on the part of sentencers may be explained by three factors:[136]

- The courts may regard female offenders as being primarily in need of treatment and support and consequently turn to a probation order to facilitate this end. This is supported by the Home Office study on the sentencing of women.

- Sentencers may be unaware of the diversity of placements available on community service and assume that the stereotypical labouring work is not appropriate for women.

- The courts may feel that community service is not a viable option for women with dependent children.

5.25   The Howard League's survey of community service provision for women shows that the low numbers of women inevitably impedes the development of specialist provision:

"...the picture that emerges is of community service units dealing with women sent to them but on a case-by-case basis."[137]

5.26   Probation services rarely provide separate community service programmes for women, largely because of the practical difficulties of finding appropriate work and supervision for small numbers of offenders. The alternative has been for women to participate in mixed work groups or to be offered an individual placement with an outside agency. The Howard League's review suggested that mixed groups appeared to work well in many cases and were said to 'normalise' the working environment. However, concern was expressed about women being placed alone in groups and earlier research has shown how male dominated groups can result in the sexual harassment of women and undermine their successful completion of the order.[138] The Howard League expressed concern about the potential for sexual harassment to be overlooked:

"...often victims will be reluctant to report incidents...staff may themselves be unwilling to bring issues to the fore, in case it adversely affects the smooth running of the group."[139]

5.27   The lack of child care arrangements was also commented upon unfavourably. Only 12 probation services, out of the 42 which participated in the study, had any projects with crèche facilities. The provision of childcare was described as 'patchy and haphazard' and whilst this was partly due to budgetary

135 Worral, A. (1997), *Punishment in the Community: The Future of Criminal Justice,* London: Longman, pp. 95-99.

136 Howard League for Penal Reform (1999), *Do Women Paint Fences Too? Women's Experience of Community Service.* London: Howard League for Penal Reform.

137 Ibid, p.18.

138 Armstrong, S. (1990), *Alternatives to Custody? Day Centre and Community Service Provision for Women,* Occasional Paper 4, University of Keele, Centre for Criminology.

139 Ibid p.11.

constraints, it was said to signify a culture that was unprepared for women and consequently unable to instil confidence in sentencers.

5.28   But the problems surrounding community service are not solely concerned with the reluctance of sentencers to use the order for women. They also relate to the way in which these relatively high-tariff sentences are differentially imposed on male and female offenders. Research has identified greater inconsistency in the use of community service for women and has revealed that women serving these orders are doing so at an earlier stage in their criminal career than the men, and have received their order for less serious offences.[140]

5.29   We conclude that there are many women sentenced to custody who could be adequately punished in the community and that there are women serving community penalties who could be dealt with by lower tariff community punishments, or by means of a financial penalty or a discharge.

5.30   Home Office figures suggest that there are no significant differences between the reconviction rates for custody and all community penalties.[141] Yet, as George Mair pointed out in his presentation to our Inquiry, research into the effectiveness of community penalties is limited and relatively unsophisticated. Evidence suggests that the reconviction rates for women who have received a community penalty are lower than for men; that there are important differences between offenders of different ages; and that different types of interventions and programmes yield different results. Clearly, the incapacitative effects of a prison sentence can only be assured for the duration of the sentence and then only if any offending behaviour in prison is discounted. Given that the majority of women received into prison are serving very short sentences, the protection that is afforded to the public is negligible.

> *"For as long as they are locked up, prison affords the greatest degree of protection to the public...However, nearly all prisoners are released at some point and at present, rarely have to confront their offending behaviour in order to be rehabilitated to the same extent as those who have taken part in the more intensive forms of probation. At this point it is not so clear that prison has protected the public in the longer term. If community sentences are effective at weaning offenders away from a criminal lifestyle, they may, in many cases, offer the most effective long-term protection of the public."*[142]

The development of research into 'what works' and the current emphasis on evidence-based practice in the probation service is to be welcomed if any consistent policy on community penalties is to be developed.

---

140   See Hine, J. (1993), 'Access for Women: Flexible and Friendly', in D. Whitfield and D. Scott (eds.), *Paying Back: Twenty Years of Community Service*, Winchester: Waterside Press; Hine, J. and Thomas, N. (1995), 'Evaluating Work with Offenders: Community Service Orders', in G. McIvor (ed.), *Working with Offenders, Research Highlights* in Social Work 26, London: Jessica Kingsley; Dominelli, L. (1984) 'Differential Justice: Domestic Labour, Community Service and Female Offenders', *Probation Journal* 31 (3) p. 100 - 103.

141   Home Office (1997), *Reconvictions of those Commencing Community Penalties in England 1993. England and Wales*, Home Office Statistical Bulletin 6/97, London: Home Office; Home Office (1997), *Reconvictions of Prisoners Discharged from Prison in 1993, England and Wales*, Home Office Statistical Bulletin 5/97, London: Home Office.

142   Home Affairs Select Committee (1998), op cit at p.xv para.45.

5.31　　The opportunities to divert women offenders from custody to punishment in the community have never been greater. The courts now have a range of penalties, supported by electronic tagging, that can restrict the liberty of the offender to a degree that was previously unattainable in a community setting. The evolution of community punishments has derived primarily from their use for male offenders. Their use for women requires further evaluation. They are potentially useful because they could enable sentencers to respond flexibly to individual offenders in terms of the need to strike a balance between reprobation, reparation and reintegration. The wide range of non-custodial penalties available makes it possible to identify categories of sanctions within which there are penalties of roughly equivalent severity.[143] But at the moment an agreed framework for such categorisation does not exist.

We recommend that an agreed framework providing guidance on the equivalent severity of categories of community penalties might be developed for the use of sentencers and that the newly established Sentencing Advisory Panel should address this issue.

5.32　　This is particularly important when considering how the courts should respond to the breach of a community order. The 1991 Criminal Justice Act introduced new procedures that distinguished those who failed to comply without reasonable excuse from those who 'wilfully and persistently' failed to comply with the conditions of their orders. What is lacking from this formulation is any principled guidance on how 'wilful persistence' is to be assessed and how the seriousness of the act of breach should relate to the original offence. Wasik and Von Hirsch have argued that although the defaulter deserves some additional punishment this should only represent a modest increase in the severity of the sanction.[144] They proposed that if a hierarchical structure of penalties existed then the breach of an order could be dealt with by imposing a penalty in the next band of severity. Without a framework of this kind there is a risk that breaches of community orders are dealt with inconsistently with one another and disproportionately to the seriousness of the original offence.

143　See Wasik, M. and Von Hirsch, A. (1988), 'Non Custodial Penalties and the Principles of Desert', *Criminal Law Review*. p.555.
144　Ibid.

5.33   The Government has now announced its Crime Reduction Strategy. While we accept the need for more rigorous and more consistent enforcement of community penalties where enforcement is necessary and justified,

> *we hope that changes to the National Standards (announced in the new Strategy) will take account of the proposal we have mentioned and will allow flexibility in cases where, for example, a mother's ability to comply with the requirements of an order is affected by her responsibility for her children.*

> *We view with great concern the proposal for social security benefits to be withdrawn from offenders who do not comply with orders, which is likely to have disproportionately severe – and unjust – consequences for many women offenders if it is applied indiscriminately to them.*

How non-custodial penalties could help reintegration

5.34   Clearly the use of community penalties provides the best possibility of a constructive approach to the needs of the offender for rehabilitation. For women, in particular, they can minimise the disruption of their family role.

5.35   The review of community disposals and the use of custody for women in Scotland identified a number of key areas in which specific provision for women needed to be made.[145] These focus on the problems that many women offenders experience in relation to drugs and alcohol dependence, previous or current abuse, the continuity and stability of accommodation and the prospects of employment. They represent a foundation upon which community facilities for women in England and Wales should be developed.

Drug and Alcohol Dependence

5.36   We have already seen (**1.38**) the scale of drug dependence among the women's prison population. The opportunities for offenders to access drug treatment in the community have been geographically uneven and the types of programme available have varied according to the idiosyncrasies of local funding arrangements and local initiatives. The introduction of the Drug Treatment and Testing Order (DTTO) provides an opportunity to direct funds toward community treatment programmes and to facilitate a broader geographical coverage. These orders are intended to be high-tariff disposals and should

145 Social Work Services and Prisons Inspectorate (1998) op.cit., Chapter 4

provide a significant opportunity for the courts to displace custody for those women offenders with drug problems who wish to abstain from further use.

5.37   Extending access to community drug treatment facilities is, in our view, an essential and urgent goal of public policy. At the moment treatment programmes in the community are in short supply and many operate with long waiting lists. The issue of 'coerced consent' to treatment, however, raises its own difficulties. A view shared by many providers of drug treatment services is that all those who will potentially receive treatment must be motivated to stop using drugs. Research evidence from the United States, on the other hand, suggests that initial motivation may not be crucial and that those receiving coerced treatment within the criminal justice system respond no less favourably than others.[146] The reality is that little is known about what types of treatment are best suited to what types of user and this raises special ethical problems when the intervention is legally coerced:

> **"Coercing a drug misuser into inappropriate treatment can arguably be regarded as a miscarriage of justice."**[147]

The DTTO does not specify the type of treatment to be provided, and passes this decision to the treatment provider. However the statutory requirements of the order clearly envisage demonstrable progress towards abstinence from all illicit drug use and this may mean that the order is inappropriate for certain individuals particularly where motivation to co-operate with treatment is questionable.

5.38   Other interesting approaches to reducing drug use and drug related crime include the Arrest Referral Schemes. Early evaluative research results are sufficiently promising for us to support their extension. But, as the authors of the report on three of the demonstration projects conclude, they have been handicapped by shortage of resources and, most importantly for us, they have insufficient information about women and ethnic minorities. They say that they suspect

> **"this reflects partly a reluctance to seek help on the part of those groups and partly a tendency of police and drug workers not to see them as potential users of drug services."**[148]

> **We recommend that, when drug rehabilitation services are planned, specific attention should be given to the special needs of women and to improving their access to necessary treatment.**

5.39   For example, in designing residential programmes, women's child care responsibilities should be taken into account and provision made for them to

146   Hough, M. (1996) *Drugs Misuse and the Criminal Justice System: A Review of the Literature*, London: Home Office, p.37.

147   Ibid p.50.

148   Home Office Drugs Prevention Initiative Paper 23; Edmunds, M. et al (1999), *Arrest Referral: Emerging Lessons from Research* London: HMSO, p.39; Home Office Drug Prevention Advisory Service *Drugs Intervention in the Criminal Justice Service, Guidance Manual* (no date).

bring their dependent children with them if that is most appropriate. Similarly, treatment facilities need to be locally based as the ability of many women to travel long distances is likely to be affected by their responsibilities for young children. The Scottish review suggested that some women may be reluctant to participate in treatment programmes run by statutory bodies, such as health or social services, because they fear that identifying themselves as problem drug users could have serious implications for the ways in which these organisations view their competence as parents. In Scotland proposals have been made to set up outreach approaches in 'neutral' settings and for greater liaison with maternity services for those misusers who are pregnant.

5.40   An obvious danger, despite an expansion in treatment facilities, is that women will continue to be in a minority and will be slotted into programmes that are heavily dominated by male participants. The extent to which this is problematic will vary according to individual sensibilities, but it is also likely to be highly dependent on the nature of the programme. Treatment facilities that involve intensive group work to explore deeply personal experiences may be unattractive to many women if they are to occur in male-dominated settings.

We recommend that some treatment programmes be dedicated exclusively to female drug misusers.

5.41   Clearly, the relatively small numbers of female offenders directed into treatment by the courts could not justify a wide geographical distribution of separate facilities. But there are other good reasons to argue for women's drug treatment facilities to be community resources used by all women and not just those who have been identified as offenders:

● It would obviate the criticism that women offenders are receiving treatment opportunities not available to other women because of shortage of facilities.

● It would break down any artificial barriers that separate the treatment needs of women drug misusers who are directed into programmes by the criminal justice system and those who come by other routes.

● It might, furthermore, facilitate continued treatment and support after the sentence or order has been completed.

The experience of sexual and violent abuse

5.42   The links between the experience of sexual and violent abuse, offending behaviour and self-harm are evident from the personal biographies of female offenders and especially women in prison. The relationship between these factors is extremely complex. It is evident, however, that the reintegrative needs of many women offenders include attention to their histories and current experience of abuse. The nature of the services required are likely to be varied and to call upon a diverse range of professional skills and expertise. For example, there may be need for therapeutic provision to enable women to make positive psychological adjustments, there may be an acute need for legal advice and assistance, or there may be a requirement for practical help in enabling the women to break free from a current situation of domestic abuse. Existing resources are spread unevenly across the country and, partly because they involve a disparate range of specialist services, they tend to operate in isolation from one another.

> **Greater co-ordination between the services which provide for the reintegrative needs of abused women offenders is essential if individual women are to address the composite nature of their situation.**

5.43   Providing therapeutic group work for women who have suffered abusive relationships is of limited value if they are unable to find refuge from ongoing domestic violence; similarly, the provision of acute relief needs to be accompanied by longer term legal protection of women's rights to property and access to children. These are facilities that are critical for the reintegration of many women offenders and, again, their utility is not limited to those individuals who have come to the attention of the criminal justice agencies. At the moment this work is mainly done by voluntary agencies and charitable trusts who should receive adequate support and state funding for the expansion of their efforts.

Mental health

5.44   The prevalence of mental health problems among women prisoners emerged as a major cause for concern (**1.35 – 1.37**) and the inadequacy of present provision for them within the prison system was detailed in **2.19 – 2.25**. We are aware of the extreme pressure which many community mental health services are experiencing at the present moment but nonetheless would argue strongly that imprisoning women simply because community facilities may refuse to take them or because no suitable services exist in the locality is unacceptable.

5.45   The Government has recently demonstrated a new determination to give high priority to mental health services by providing an extra £700 million of resources over the next three years to the NHS, to support policies in the White Paper *Modernising Mental Health Services* and by laying down standards for the provision of services now set out in the recently published *National Service Framework*.

We recommend that the NHS and the Prison Service joint task force should give priority to the expansion of mental health facilities for treatment in the community designed for women offenders, the majority of whom pose no threat to the public (but more often to themselves).

Accommodation

5.46   A key element in the reintegration of women offenders lies in protecting their existing accommodation. One of the most severe, yet unintended, consequences of imprisonment for many women is the loss of their home and the difficulties this creates for the re-establishment of their families after their release.

5.47   Community penalties are preferable to custody because they do not threaten the security of a woman's tenure. At the same time they may impose severe restrictions on her liberty. At the upper end of the tariff the courts may impose a 12 hour curfew with electronic monitoring and a full working day under supervision. The introduction of the electronic tag has been controversial, with some critics claiming that it violates the personal integrity of the offender. Undoubtedly it is a highly intrusive device but one that may, in our view, be justified if it facilitates the principle of parsimony in delivering punishment.

5.48   There are, however, many women offenders who do not have secure or acceptable accommodation to protect and for whom a home curfew would be entirely inappropriate. This is particularly significant where a woman is at risk of domestic violence. In these cases alternative accommodation is needed which is capable of imposing the necessary restrictions on liberty whilst offering reintegrative and restorative opportunities. Traditionally, hostels have provided this type of accommodation but there are few catering exclusively for women and especially for women with dependent children or those with particular problems such as drug dependence or mental disorder. We were impressed by the efforts made at Crowley House, a probation hostel in the West Midlands, to remove many of the obstacles that can stand in the way of women being granted hostel places. In our view, women's access to community penalties, and the effectiveness of punishment in the community, hinges on the basic accommodation needs of these women being met.

We believe that no woman should be denied punishment in the community because her home environment is too perilous, or inadequate in other ways, to enable her to serve a community penalty. The same argument applies to those women at risk of losing their liberty whilst remanded and awaiting trial or sentence.

Employment

5.49   Training programmes in women's prisons have rarely been aimed at getting women into employment on release and are hampered by the frequent transfer from one prison to another (often with different policies) and by the shortness of the sentences (**2.37 – 2.38**). We welcome the recent reassurance (in correspondence) from the Women's Policy Group that "education, training and employment opportunities now better reflect the resettlement needs of women". This is an area where continuous close monitoring is required. Women serving their sentences in the community are in a better position and a longer-term perspective could be more realistically adopted. Community penalties can provide women with links to training facilities that both in the short and longer term may help to free them from the poverty of welfare dependence.

* * * * * * * * * * * * * *

5.50   We have argued that the opportunities for reprobation, reparation and reintegration through punishment in the community are considerable. In the next chapter we consider ways in which community penalties might be co-ordinated for female offenders. We recognise, however, that there will be cases where a custodial penalty is unavoidable, either because the offence is so serious that the requirement for reprobation demands it or because the need to protect the public from serious harm requires conditions of restraint only possible in a custodial setting.

6 **Reintegration and Inclusion**

6.1   At the end of **Chapter 2**, we argued that full recognition should be given to the repercussions from the criminal justice system on the likely success of any programme to reduce social exclusion. No further research is needed to show that many of the women currently in prison should not be there nor that the consequence of them being imprisoned is socially destructive. But, however we punish women offenders - whether by placing them in custody or by imposing community penalties - the aim must be to reintegrate them as far as possible into a lifestyle which they and their families can sustain once their sentence is completed. In this chapter we begin by describing what we see as the essential elements of any programme for achieving such reintegration and how they might be organised for those women serving community sentences.

6.2   We will also argue that some similar provision is required for those who will be held in custody. There would then be the possibility of linking custodial with community provision, so as to provide a pathway for sentence planning and a transition from custody to community towards the end of a sentence.

6.3   What would be the components of an integrated approach which could provide the rehabilitation experience appropriate to the needs of women offenders and to their offending patterns? An admirable summary has been provided in *Women Offenders – A Safer Way*[149] and we reproduce this diagrammatic presentation:

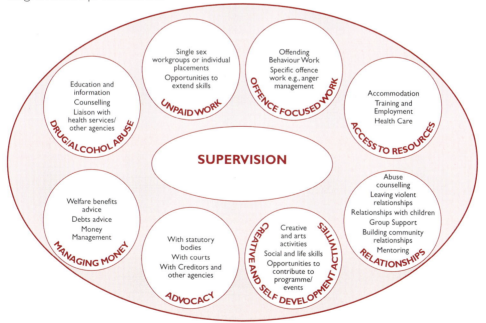

149   Social Work Services and Prisons Inspectorates for Scotland (1998), op. cit. p.38.

6.4   Supervision is central. It would be in the hands of the Probation Service. (It has been suggested that the name of the service is about to be changed to Community Punishment and Rehabilitation Service. In the light of our proposals below - that the co-ordinated services we wish to see provided to offenders, with supervision by probation, should also be available without supervision to non-offenders - we would view such a change as unfortunate).

Community support centres

6.5   The provision of the necessary services, linked to supervision, will involve the participation of a wide range of other agencies extending well beyond the criminal justice system – to include local authorities, the health and employment services as well as voluntary bodies.

To provide for the necessary co-ordination and management of services, we recommend that a national network of Women's Supervision, Rehabilitation and Support Centres should be established.

6.6   As well as the supervision of court orders, the Centres would provide access, either directly under the same roof or by referral agreements with community agencies, to a wide range of services. If this proposal appears ambitious, it must be remembered that it is wholly consistent with the Government's declared objective of 'joined-up services'. Initiatives are already under way in other policy areas to facilitate genuine 'joint working' - for example the new power given to Health and Local Authorities to pool some budgets. The approach is also consistent with that adopted in projects aimed at reducing social exclusion, such as the Single Regeneration Budgets, Health Action Zones and Sure Start programmes. Our proposal leaves room for experimentation and adaptation to local circumstances.

> *Our recommendation is that, building on existing experience, plans should be drawn up for the establishment in geographically accessible centres of a network of Women's Supervision, Rehabilitation and Support Centres.*

A practical example

6.7   A practical example of this approach which has impressed us is the Women Offender Programme, initiated by the Hereford and Worcester Probation Service in 1993. Its scope is limited to provision for women offenders under supervision in the community. The aim is to help women avoid further offending by increasing their abilities to solve complex problems legitimately: by holding in balance the demands made upon them, the external resources and legitimate opportunities available to them, and their own capacities and abilities.

6.8   The programme is intended to be applicable to the majority of women given probation or combination orders, as well as catering for women with more serious records of offending and subject to the requirements of parole licences. Women can gain direct access to other services beyond the Probation Service and the programme serves as a focal point for networking and as a forum for group work. Judith Rumgay, an academic consultant to the project, identified two conceptual strands that guided the development of practice:

"One of these was 'normalisation', which encouraged an effort to reduce female offenders' isolation from community based networks of support. The second, complementary strand was to reduce the emphasis on the probation service as a focal resource for women who were seen to have social and personal needs in common with many non-offending women."[150]

6.9   We have been encouraged by the decision of the Home Office to fund the Hereford and Worcester programme in the first round of the 'pathfinder' projects. These projects are to be evaluated with a view to developing accredited programmes based on empirical evidence of 'What Works'.[151]

Networks

6.10   There are many clear advantages in approaching the reintegrative needs of women offenders through developing a network of community based centres:

● access to services can, where appropriate, be continued after any sentences have been completed. This would enable the length of programmes to be determined by their content rather than by the length of sentence;

● some programmes could be made available on a voluntary basis to non-offenders from similar backgrounds and with similar problems. In this way the programmes could serve a preventative purpose;

● the centres could be encouraged to develop in such a way as to provide a supportive "community" of women which might offer an alternative to the often criminogenic environment or isolation into which so many women offenders return on completion of their sentences. This would help to reduce the risk of re-offending. These networks of support should make it possible for the women to establish other frames of reference within their own location. Of particular value would be the access that women could have to self-help groups and the opportunities provided for mentoring in relation to issues such as drug misuse, violent and sexual abuse and racial harassment;

---

150   Rumgay J. (1999) Paper presented to Committee Seminar on 9 February 1999. See also Rumgay, J. (2000), Improving User Participation and Involvement.

151   Probation Circular 35/98 *Effective Practice Initiative – A national implementation plan for the effective supervision of offenders* stated that the Association of Chief Officers of Probation, HM Inspector of Probation and the Home Office would be working with Probation areas to develop a portfolio of high quality 'pathfinder' programmes which incorporate 'What Works Principles'. The pathfinder programmes will lead to the development of accredited programmes based on empirical evidence of 'what works'.

● the protection of family ties, particularly in relation to the maintenance of contact with children, would foster the re-integration of the offender while reducing harmful consequences for the family, upon which we place so much emphasis. There is much scope here, for experimentation and adaptation to local circumstances.

Custodial Provision

6.11   The adoption of this integrated model of provision for community sentences still leaves open the question of how to deal with the population of women offenders for whom some form of custodial facility would be essential. The present structure of relatively large, self-contained institutions that are sparsely distributed across the country will become even less appropriate as the population of female prisoners is reduced. Other commentators have addressed this question and reached similar conclusions, namely that the existing system of women's prisons should be dismantled and replaced by smaller secure units, serving a relatively local community.[152] In his *Thematic Review*, Sir David Ramsbotham speaks of 'urban prisons' and draws on one example at Shakopee, Minnesota in the U.S.A. where

"prisoners serving very long sentences, for very serious offences, are held alongside prisoners serving short sentences, in a prison without a perimeter fence".

Prisoners nearing the end of their sentences, subject to security risks, progress to a transitional urban establishment from where they can attend community facilities, seek employment etc. This half-way house contains both women who have been sentenced to custody and others who are serving probation sentences and requiring residency. There is also an attempt to link offenders with community resources. Sir David's comment was that

"this example can provide valuable lessons for the United Kingdom's approach to offending behaviour by throughcare for women prisoners."[153]

We recommend that a programme should be prepared, costed and time-tabled for the replacement of existing women's prisons with suitable, geographically dispersed, custodial centres.

Links with local support centres?

6.12   It is for discussion how closely some secure units should be linked with the proposed Support Centres. It could certainly be argued that they should be

152   Learmont, J. (1995), *Review of Prison Service Security in England and Wales and the Escape from Parkhurst Prison on Tuesday 3rd January 1995*, Cm 3020, London: HMSO; Woolf, H. and Tumim, S. (1991) op. cit .

153   HM Chief Inspector of Prisons (1997), op. cit. para. 3.17-3.21 and para. 11.52-11.56

geographically distinct, as in the American example above. Some people might argue that any association between the resource centres and the secure units would make it less attractive for community agencies to ally themselves with the enterprise and for non-offending women, who could benefit from the services, to join voluntarily. But there can be no doubt that whatever the physical nature and location of the custodial provision, far more resources must be devoted to the rehabilitative programmes provided within custody than is currently the case. As with community provision, this conclusion is based upon evidence of effectiveness.

How secure is secure?

6.13   This is an appropriate point to raise the question of the nature of the security to be provided in the secure units. To adopt standards set in the male prison system is difficult to justify, given the different risk profiles of the populations (**Chapter 1**) and the fact that, in the event of a successful attempt to escape, few women have the contacts and resources to evade the criminal justice system permanently. Indeed it could be argued that under our proposed custodial arrangements the main impetus that drives women to abscond - a desire to get home to sort out a problem within the family - could be assuaged by providing inmates with greater opportunities to keep more closely in touch with their domestic responsibilities. We would agree with Sir David Rasmbotham's opinion that what he calls effective procedural measures can meet the needs of security and control in most cases.[154]

6.14   A particular problem concerns the detention of women serving long sentences. First there are 'lifers'. The three women released on life licence in 1997 served an average of 16.7 years in prison.[155] Sentence planning is supposed to be geared to the periodic transfer of these women to different establishments, in an effort to avoid individual stagnation and institutionalisation and to offer some sense of development. But in the *Thematic Review* Sir David says that

> **"sentence planning for women serving life sentences is inadequate ... Many women did not have a plan at all... The risk assessment model used (which is based on adult males serving life sentences) is inappropriate..."**[156]

So one must conclude that the present system for lifers is unsatisfactory. We would not deny that this population raises difficult issues. However, we are not convinced that these are insurmountable, particularly when looked at in the context of our broader sentencing reforms. The overwhelming majority of women lifers are serving a mandatory sentence for murder. We endorse the recommendations made by the Committee on the Penalty for Homicide and the proposal to abolish mandatory life sentences for murder and to give the courts the discretion to impose determinate sentences.[157] For women serving long terms, the concept of career progression should be retained but its expression

154   HM Chief Inspector of Prisons (1997i), op. cit. para 5.06.

155   Data provided by Home Office on 10 February 2000. As only two or three women are released each year on life licence, it is impossible to arrive at a figure of average time served. In 1995, the average time served was 10.9 years, in 1996 it was 12 years and in 1997 it was 16.7 years.

156   HM Chief Inspector of Prisons (1997), op. cit. paras 11.10 – 12.

157   House of Lords (1989), *Report of the Select Committee on Murder and Life Imprisonment*, (House of Lords Paper 78, 1988 – 1989.) London: HMSO.

could be found in the development of skills and community links, as well as in geographical relocation if that is desirable.

Women who are foreign nationals

6.15   There is one other major category of long-term prisoners: women who are foreign nationals serving relatively long determinate sentences for drug offences. As we have already discussed, the deterrent purpose of sentencing these women to long periods of custody has not been evaluated and its effectiveness must be highly questionable. In their cases, achieving the objectives of reprobation, reintegration and reparation poses an insurmountable problem of balance since reintegration into their own communities cannot be a realistic objective, given their long distance from home.

> **The Government, with advice from the Criminal Justice Consultative Council, should as a matter of urgency consider the policy questions raised by women who are foreign nationals serving relatively long determinate sentences.**

Can we afford it?

6.16   Our proposals face the likely criticism that they are not only resource intensive and disproportionately expensive but also make demands upon services in the community which are already under pressure. This argument has to be set alongside the true costs of imprisonment, not simply in terms of the expenditure incurred in running the female estate but also the indirect financial and social costs associated with the care of children and the longer term consequences of family dislocation.[158] The financial viability of our proposals is predicated on the phased closure of women's prisons as they are currently organised. Failure to close existing establishments would mean that secure accommodation would displace non-custodial penalties and thus leave unchanged the existing tendency to imprison women. Here the principle of accountability is important, in that the costs of our proposals should be evaluated against their outcomes and the extent to which they are effective in delivering their objectives.

6.17   We believe that in the medium term and certainly in the long term, our proposals will be cost effective. But we are in no doubt that it will require an injection of resources to bridge the start-up costs of the new local support centres before any savings can be realised from the closure of traditional prisons. And these, in turn, will require additional resources for the essential upgrading of regimes, health services etc. Moreover the co-ordination and re-training required to deliver effectively the range of services and facilities required of the custody and support centres will itself take time and hence resources.

---

158   Wolfe, T. (1998) op. cit.

6.18   We recognise that it will be some time before sentencing practice will respond to our call for change and before the number of women being sentenced to custody will be significantly reduced. It may also be several years before those who still receive custodial sentences can be accommodated in small community prisons. We recognise the obstacles to the rapid creation of a network of Supervision, Rehabilitation and Support Centres not only in funding, but also in finding suitable sites, overcoming local opposition, and obtaining planning consent. It will therefore be essential to ensure, first, that a programme of creating local centres is pressed forward with political determination and administrative energy and skill and, secondly, that the necessary reforms are made in the management of those women's prisons that will remain in use in the short and medium term.

6.19   We are conscious that structural changes can distract effort from the day-to-day management of a service and from the practical objectives which the changes are themselves intended to achieve. The reorganisation of public services - in health, education, the prison system itself - has too often been seen as a solution to a problem rather than the preparation which has to be made before a solution can be attempted. But we believe that the problem of women's imprisonment has become too serious for progress to be made within the existing administrative structure and that a radical structural reform is now needed, comparable with the reform which the Government has introduced in the system of youth justice.

The Way Forward

6.20   We conclude therefore that a new separate authority, with its own budget and management structure is needed to oversee the arrangements for women's imprisonment and punishment in the community; to provide the driving force to establish local centres; to develop programmes based in communities; and to ensure that prisons for women are efficiently and humanely managed to provide suitable conditions and regimes. The authority would also be charged with the responsibility for ensuring that programmes, whether provided in custody or in the community, achieve not only their quantified targets or outputs (such as the places made available or the numbers completing particular programmes), but also satisfactory social outcomes in terms of settlement, integration, and reduced offending. The location of such an authority - within the criminal justice system - would be parallel to that of the National Youth Justice Board, and it is for discussion whether it should report direct to Parliament or via the Home Secretary.

6.21   As a Committee of Inquiry we do not have the capacity to spell out the details of what would be involved in such a major upheaval in the system of dealing with women offenders. We can however indicate the main direction in which we are convinced the Government should move. To take our proposals forward with the speed that we believe the problem demands, we recommend:

the immediate establishment of a statutory commissioning body – the National Women's Justice Board – charged with producing a plan for action within the next 2 years.

7 Conclusions and Recommendations

7.1   The starting point for our inquiry was the rapid increase in the number of women prisoners during the mid-1990s. We soon realised that this increase was not just a reflection of the general increase in the prison population during that period but a symptom of a much more fundamental fault in the country's arrangements for dealing with women offenders as a whole. It may not be as visible but is certainly just as serious in its immediate and longer term consequences as the crisis in youth justice which the Government made one of its first priorities when it came into office. It demands an equally radical approach.

7.2   The fault is the consequence of the failure of the criminal justice system to acknowledge those characteristics of women who offend and the nature of their offences which are distinct from men. This failure has rendered the structures, methods and practices – indeed the underlying mindset of the whole system – unsuitable and often inequitable for women. Equal treatment – which we fully endorse – does not mean identical treatment, whether for women or for members of cultural or ethnic minorities. In the prison system women prisoners have suffered from the well-intentioned attempts to 'impose equality' (and standardisation) and to promote the unity of the Prison Service. And throughout the criminal justice system women offenders have been disadvantaged by a failure to recognise both the degree of deprivation which characterises the backgrounds of so many and the wider consequences of custodial sentences for them and their families (**Chapter 1**). We conclude that a government seriously concerned to reduce social exclusion cannot ignore the repercussions from the criminal justice system, as it currently operates, upon other social policies. There is, therefore, an overwhelming case for a reduction in the use of imprisonment for such women offenders (**Chapter 2**).

7.3   These considerations then led us to examine the principles of punishment currently prevailing in the criminal justice system and to conclude that, in important respects, they present a framework which is both limited and confusing. We therefore felt required to articulate the principles which we believe must underpin society's response to offending whether by men or women. We identified three fundamentals. The first is the principle of citizenship: that the criminal justice system should foster respect for the rights and responsibilities of citizenship and provide for the potential realisation of those rights to the greatest extent compatible with a similar possibility for all other citizens. The second is the evaluation by social outcomes: that criminal justice policy should be judged in terms of its social outcomes and that these outcomes should be closely monitored and evaluated through research. The third is joined-up, integrated policy-making: criminal justice policy should always be consistent with the whole spectrum of criminal justice and social policy objectives, and in particular, with the effort to reduce structural social exclusion. Building on these fundamentals, we argue that the main rationale for punishment consists in the objectives of reprobation - penal censure and harsh treatment where necessary, but proportionate to the seriousness of the offence; reparation to victims and the community; and reintegration – the provision of opportunities for integration and the minimisation of long term stigmatisation. The aim of penal policies and penal practices should be to make these objectives compatible with one another and to strike a balance between them wherever they conflict. Further, we argue that state punishment should respect the principles of parsimony: the state should inflict the smallest amount of punishment adequate to protect the community from crime; non-discrimination: all practices and principles of punishment should be such as to be capable of being applied in a non-discriminatory way to all citizens irrespective of sex, racial, ethnic, religious, class or other differences; and accountability: all practices should be subject to democratic processes of accountability (**Chapter 3**).

7.4   Against this background - on the one hand of the reality of the nature of women offenders, and on the other, of the theoretical justifications for punishing them - we examine the operation of current sentencing policy. We conclude that a return to the basic framework of sentencing set out in the Criminal Justice Act 1991 could, with elaboration of some further guidelines, provide a basis for the consistent sentencing of women. In particular it would result in custodial sentences being imposed only where the offence is so serious that such a penalty alone could adequately reflect the necessary degree of reprobation or where custody is necessary to protect the public from harm (**Chapter 4**).

7.5   We then address the question of how the criminal justice system should provide for those women who, after the application of the principles advocated in 7.3 above, (and in detail in **Chapter 3**) still merit punishment. We conclude that the opportunities for punishment in the community have never been greater but that an agreed framework and guidance as to their use is required. We also argue that both custodial and non-custodial sentences must be accompanied by programmes designed to facilitate the reintegration of women offenders and, where appropriate, their dependants, into a sustainable and non-offending lifestyle (**Chapter 5**).

7.6   We have surveyed the available evidence to determine the essential elements of such an integrated approach. We conclude that a radical restructuring is required both of the way in which policy for women offenders is determined and of the way in which it is delivered. In **Chapter 6** we make our central recommendation:

A National Women's Justice Board should be established immediately as a statutory commissioning body which would resemble in many respects the National Youth Justice Board.

Summary of Recommendations

1.   Structure

We recommend that:

The National Women's Justice Board should be established forthwith as a separate authority, charged with the development and implementation of policy for women offenders, consistent with the principles enunciated above. The Board should control its own budget and management structure and should possess powers to commission from other relevant agencies – including the Prison Service, the NHS, local authorities and voluntary bodies – the services required to provide the necessary programmes of supervision, rehabilitation and reintegration.

It should also be charged with the establishment and management of:

(i)   a network of local Women's Supervision, Rehabilitation and Support Centres to provide an effective supervision and rehabilitation service to offenders who are serving community sentences;

(ii)   a national system of geographically dispersed custodial units to replace the existing women's prison system, taking advice from, among others, the existing Prison Service. These should be linked to the Women's Supervision, Rehabilitation and Support Centres through the sharing of rehabilitative and other services where appropriate and as a pathway for sentence planning.

(iii)   in the inevitable transition period before all these custodial units are in place, the remaining women's prisons.

Firm plans should be available within two years for implementing these recommendations.

2.   Sentencing

We recommend that:

(i)   the Court of Appeal, with advice from the Sentencing Advisory Panel, should articulate a fresh interpretation of the requirements of the Criminal Justice Act 1991 upon which sentencing should proceed, in accordance with the principles of reprobation, reparation and reintegration set out above. It should emphasise the need for sentencing to be rational, consistent and transparent (**4.29**);

(ii) consideration be given to amending the Sentencing Advisory Panel's statutory basis in the light of the recommendation we make for expanding its work (**4.15**);

(iii) the Sentencing Advisory Panel should be invited to develop a framework providing guidance on the equivalent severity of categories of community penalties (**5.31**);

(iv) consideration should be given to the reintroduction of a system of unit fines (**4.19**);

(v) the distinctive position of women offenders should be taken into account in determination of sentence and the Court of Appeal and the Sentencing Advisory Panel should consider mitigating factors which might be of particular significance for women (**4.18**);

(vi) courts should always consider carefully a pre-sentence report in any case involving a women offender where a custodial or community sentence may be in prospect (**4.20**);

(vii) the piloting of reprimands and warnings (as introduced for young offenders) should be extended to adults to enable an element of restorative justice to be incorporated in adult diversions;

(viii) the courts should be entitled and encouraged to report to the Home Office if they consider the facilities to be provided under the terms of a court order are inadequate (**4.28**);

(ix) part I of the Crime (Sentences) Act 1997 should be immediately repealed. (**4.29**).

3.   The Principle of Accountability

We recommend that:

(i) the Criminal Justice Consultative Council should be integrated with the Government's own machinery for strategic planning and joined-up policy across the criminal justice system (**4.31**);

(ii) data about state punishment and of its financial cost should be gathered regularly, and published (**3.19**);

(iii) properly funded, independent inspectorates should be developed to monitor all areas of penal practice (**3.19**);

(iv) these inspectorates should be invested with sufficient power to ensure that their recommendations are implemented (**3.19**).

4.   Minimising the use of custody

We recommend that:

(i)   diversion should be increased for women charged with offences of low seriousness, particularly for those suffering from mental health problems (**5.13**);

(ii)   existing provision for community penalties, co-ordinated through the newly established network of Women's Supervision, Rehabilitation and Support Centres, should be used more extensively and should be refocused to make them more relevant to women offenders (**5.15**);

(iii)   there should be a systematic exploration of bail decisions with a view to reducing the use of custodial remand in the light of the Law Commission's recommendation for review of parts of the Bail Act (**5.5**);

(iv)   steps should be taken to ensure that cautioning is used more systematically to achieve consistency and equitable treatment (**5.12**);

5.   Custodial Regimes

We recommend that:

(i)   urgent consideration should be given to improving arrangements for prison visits and, in particular, temporary release, to support and facilitate the maintenance of family ties of women in custody (**2.29 – 2.30**);

(ii)   women held in custodial accommodation should be given access to the same range of reintegrative facilities as will be provided for women serving community sentences (**6.2**);

(iii)   the steps currently being taken by the Women's Policy Group to ensure that all existing women's prisons can offer accredited education and training provision, and offending behaviour programmes, are monitored and evaluated (**5.49**);

(iv)   adherence to the principle that women should not be separated from their babies in prison, except in exceptional circumstances, should be central to policy for this group of women and that the implementation of the Prison Service Standards, which it is proposed will incorporate most of the recommendations from the Mother and Babies Report, should be closely monitored (See **Introduction**).

6.   Health

We recommend that:

(i)   the joint task force of the Prison Service and the NHS should give priority to major improvements in the quality of health care provision in custodial settings and for offenders serving community sentences (**2.24**);

(ii)   an audit of patterns of drug prescribing be undertaken within women's prisons with a view to developing, jointly with the NHS, a protocol of best practice, the implementation of which should be monitored by the NHS (**2.25**);

(iii)   immediate improvements should be made in drug treatment facilities for women offenders both in custody (**2.26**) and in the community (**5.38**) and that some treatment programmes in the community should be dedicated exclusively to female drug misusers (**5.39**);

(iv)   there should be greater co-ordination between services to provide for the reintegrative needs of women offenders who have suffered violent and/or sexual abuse (**5.41**);

(v)   the NHS and Prison Service joint task force should give priority to the expansion of mental health facilities for treatment in the community, designed for women offenders (**5.45**).

7.   Foreign National Women in Prison

We recommend that:

(i)   the Government, with advice from the Criminal Justice Consultative Council, should, as a matter of urgency, consider the policy issues raised by women who are foreign nationals serving relatively long determinate sentences (**6.15**).

8.   The need for further research

We recommend that research is undertaken:

(i)   to analyse the sentencing of women, paying particular attention to the nature of the offence and the social characteristics of the offender, in particular, ethnicity and age (**1.9-1.10**);

(ii)   on the quality and consistency of pre-sentence reports and on their use by the courts (**4.20**);

(iii)   on how and why remand decisions are reached and the reasons for refusing bail (**5.4-5.5**);

(iv)   on the availability and use of court diversion schemes and of their outcomes (**5.13**);

(v)   on the relative effectiveness of different forms of community penalties
        (compared with custody) (**5.29-5.30**);

(vi)   on the effectiveness of Arrest Referral Schemes for drug misusers (**5.36**);

(vii)   on the needs of mentally disordered female offenders, the nature of their
        offences and the problems which arise for the criminal justice system and
        health services in responding to their needs and offending behaviour (**5.45**);

(viii) to measure the effects of custody on women's mental health (**4.18**).

(ix)   Finally we would wish to see our own recommendation for the
        establishment of Women's Supervision, Rehabilitation and Support Centres
        and of small Custodial Units subjected to a rigorous system of evaluation.

References

Allen, H. (1987), *Justice Unbalanced*, Oxford: Oxford University Press.

Armstrong, S. (1990), *Alternatives to Custody? Day Centre and Community Service Provision for Women*, Occasional Paper 4, University of Keele, Centre for Criminology.

Ashworth, A. (1998), The Criminal Process: *An Evaluative Study* (2nd edition), Oxford: Oxford University Press.

Ashworth, A. (1995), *Sentencing and Criminal Justice* (2nd edition), London: Butterworths.

Ashworth, A. and Player, E. (1998), 'Sentencing, Equal Treatment and the Impact of Sanctions' in A. Ashworth and M. Wasik (eds.), *Fundamentals of Sentencing Theory*, Oxford: Oxford University Press.

Baverstock (1993), *14 Criminal Appeal Reports 371*.

Bentham, J. (1983, first published 1789), *An Introduction to the Principles of Morals and Legislation*, London: Methuen.

Bexley (1993), *14 Criminal Appeal Reports 462*.

Braithwaite, J. (1989), *Crime, Shame and Reintegration*, Cambridge: Cambridge University Press.

Braithwaite, J. and Daly, K. (1994), 'Masculinities and Communitarian Control' in T. Newburn and E. Stanko (eds.), *Just Boys Doing Business*, London: Routledge.

Braithwaite, J. and Pettit, P. (1990), *Not Just Deserts*, Oxford: Clarendon Press.

Burney, E. and Pearson, G. (1995), 'Mentally Disordered Offenders: Finding a Focus for Diversion', *Howard Journal of Criminal Justice*, vol. 34.

Burns, J.H. and Hart, H.L.A. (1983), *An Introduction to the Principles of Morals and Legislation*, London: Methuen.

Caddle, D. and Crisp, D. (1997), *Imprisoned Women and Mothers*, Home Office Research Study 162, London: Home Office.

Carlen, P. (1998), *Sledgehammer: Women's Imprisonment at the Millennium*, London: Macmillan.

Carlen, P. (1983), *Women's Imprisonment*, London: Routledge.

Carson, D. (1989), 'Prosecuting People with Mental Handicaps', *Criminal Law Review*, p.87.

Crime (Sentences) Act 1997.

Crime and Disorder Act 1998.

Criminal Justice Act 1991.

Cunningham (1993), 96 Criminal Appeal Reports 422.

Department of Health (1998), *Modernising Mental Health Services*, London: HMSO.

Daly, K. and Tonry, M. (1997), 'Gender Race and Sentencing' in M. Tonry (ed.), *Crime and Justice: A Review of Research*, vol. 22.

Devlin, A. (1998), *Invisible Women*, Winchester: Waterside Press.

Dominelli, L. (1984), 'Differential Justice: Domestic Labour, Community Service and Female Offender', *Probation Journal*, vol. 31 (3).

Duff, R.A. (1999), *Punishment and Society.*

Duff, R.A. (1986), *Trials and Punishments*, Cambridge: Cambridge University Press.

Eaton, M. (1986), *Justice for Women*, Oxford: Oxford University Press.

Edmunds, M. *et al* (1999), *Arrest Referral: Emerging Lessons from Research*, Drugs Prevention Initiative, Paper 23, London: HMSO.

Evans, R. (1993), *The Conduct of Police Interviews with Juveniles*, Royal Commission on Criminal Justice, Study no.8.

Farrington, D. and Morris, A. (1989), 'Sex, Sentencing and Reconvictions', *British Journal of Criminology*, vol. 229.

Fitzgerald, M. (1993), *Ethnic Minorities and the Criminal Justice System*, Royal Commission on Criminal Justice, Research Study no.20.

Flood-Page, C. and Mackie, A. (1998), *Sentencing Practice: an examination of decisions in Magistrates Courts in the mid-1990s*, Home Office Research, Study 180.

Flynn, N. (1998), *Introduction to Prisons and Imprisonment*, Winchester: Waterside Press.

Hedderman, C. and Dowds, L. (1997), *The Sentencing of Women, a section 95 publication*, Home Office Research Findings no.58.

Hedderman, C. and Gelsthorpe, L. (1997), *Understanding the Sentencing of Women*, Home Office Research, Study no.170.

Hedderman, C. and Hough, M. (1994), 'Does the Criminal Justice System Treat Men and Women Differently?', Home Office Research Findings no.10.

Hine, J. and Thomas, N. (1995), 'Evaluating Work with Offenders: Community Service Orders' in G. McIvor (ed.), *Working with Offenders: Research Highlights in Social Work 26*, London: Jessica Kingsley.

Hine, J. (1993), 'Access for Women: Flexible and Friendly' in D. Whitfield and D. Scott (eds.), *Paying Back: Twenty Years of Community Service*, Waterside Press: Winchester.

H.M. Chief Inspector of Prisons for England and Wales (1999), *HMP Brockhill – Report of a Full Inspection*, London: Home Office.

H. M. Chief Inspector of Prisons for England and Wales (1997i), *Women in Prison - a thematic review*, London: Home Office.

H.M. Chief Inspector of Prisons for England and Wales (1997ii), *HMP Highpoint – Report of a Full Inspection*, London: Home Office.

H.M. Prison Service (1999i), *Annual Report and Accounts April 1998 - March 1999*, London: Home Office.

H.M. Prison Service (1999ii), *The Future Organisation of Prison Health Care*, London: Home Office.

H.M. Prison Service (1994), *Health Care Standards for Prisons in England and Wales*, London: Home Office.

H.M. Treasury (1999), *The Modernisation of Britain's Tax and Benefit System No.4 - Tackling Poverty and Extending Opportunity*, London: Home Office.

Hobcraft, J. and Kiernan, K. (1999), *Childhood Poverty, Early Motherhood and Adult Social Exclusion*, Working Paper 28, LSE Centre for the Analysis of Social Exclusion.

Hobcraft, J. (1998), *Intergenerational and Life Course Transmission of Social Exclusion*, Working Paper 15, LSE Centre for the Analysis of Social Exclusion.

Home Affairs Select Committee (1998), *Third Report: Alternatives to Prison Sentences*, London: HMSO.

Home Office (1999i), *Prison Statistics England and Wales 1998*, London: HMSO.

Home Office (1999ii), *Prison Population Brief*, London: HMSO.

Home Office (1999iii), *Prison Population Brief England and Wales: June 1999*, London: HMSO.

Home Office (1999iv), *Women in the Criminal Justice System: a section 95 publication*, London: HMSO.

Home Office (1998), *Prison Statistics England and Wales 1997*.

Home Office (1997i), *Aspects of Crime and Gender*, London: Home Office.

Home Office (1997ii), *Reconvictions of those Commencing Community Penalties in England 1993*, Home Office Statistical Bulletin 5/97.

Home Office (1997iii), *Reconvictions of Prisoners Discharged from Prison in 1993*, Home Office Statistics Bulletin 5/97.

Home Office, Police and Criminal Evidence Act 1984, Codes of Practice (3rd edition 1995) Code D.

Home Office (1995), *Review of Prison Service Security in England and Wales and the Escape from Parkhurst Prison on Tuesday 3 January*, cm 3020, London: HMSO.

Home Office (1994), *The Escape from Whitemoor Prison on Friday September 24*, cm 2741, London HMSO.

Home Office (1990), *Crime, Justice and Protecting the Public,* London: HMSO, para 4.3.

Home Office Drug Prevention Advisory Service (Undated), *Drugs Intervention in the Criminal Justice Service*, Guidance Manual.

Honderich, T. (1976), *Punishment: the Supposed Justifications*, Cambridge: Polity Press.

Hood, R. with Cordoril, G. (1992), *Race and Sentencing: a Study in the Crown Courts*, Oxford: Clarendon Press.

Hough, M. (1996), *Drug Misuse and the Criminal Justice System: A Review of the Literature*, London: Home Office.

Hough, M. (1995), 'Scotching a Fallacy: Are the courts tougher on women than men?', *Criminal Justice Matters*, vol. 22.

House of Lords (1989), *Report of the Select Committee on Murder and Life Imprisonment.*

Howard League for Penal Reform (1999), *Do Women Paint Fences Too? Women's Experience of Community Service*, London: Howard League for Penal Reform.

Hudson, B. (1988), 'Mitigation for Socially Deprived Offenders' in A. Von Hirsch and A. Ashworth *Principled Sentencing*, Oxford: Hart Publishing.

Hudson, B. (1998), 'Doing Justice to Difference' in A. Ashworth and M. Wasik, eds. *Fundamentals of Sentencing Theory*, Oxford: Oxford University Press.

Hudson, B. (1998), 'Restorative Justice: The Challenge of Sexual and Racial Violence', *Journal of Law and Society*, 25 pp.237-256.

Jefferson, T. and Walker, M. (1992), 'Ethnic Minorities in the Criminal Justice System', *Criminal Law Review.*

Kegan, P., Farrington, D. and Morris, A. (1983), 'Sex, Sentencing and Conviction', *British Journal of Criminology* 23, pp 229-248.

Kennedy, H. (1993), *Eve Was Framed: Women and British Justice*, London: Chatto & Windus.

Lacey, N. (1988), *State Punishment: Political Principles and Community Values,* London: Routledge.

Lyon, J. and Coleman, J. (1996), *Understanding and Working with Young Women in Custody.* HM Prison Service Training Pack. Brighton: Trust for the Study of Adolescence.

Maden, A., Swinton, M. and Gunn, J. (1994), 'A Criminological and Psychiatric Survey of Women Serving a Prison Sentence', *British Journal of Criminology*, 34.

Morris, A., Wilkinson, C., Tisi, A., Woodrow, J. and Rockley, A. (1995), *Managing the Needs of Female Prisoners*, London: Home Office.

Morris, N. and Tonry, M. (1990), *Between Prison and Probation: Intermediate Punishments in a Rational Sentencing System*, New York: Oxford University Press.

Morris, N. (1974), *The Future of Imprisonment*, Chicago: University of Chicago Press.

Moxon, D. (1989), *Sentencing Practice in the Crown Courts*, Home Office Research Study no. 103.

Penal Affairs Consortium (1996), *The Imprisonment of Women: Some Facts and Figures.*

Prison Reform Trust (1997), *Sentencing: A Geographical Lottery*, London: Prison Reform Trust.

Prison Service (1999), *Report of a Review of Principles, Policies and Procedures on Mothers and Babies in Prison*, London: Home Office.

Probation Circular 35/98, *Effective Practice Initiative - A national implementation plan for the effective supervision of offenders.*

Rutherford, A. (1986), *Prisons and the Process of Justice*, Oxford: Oxford University Press.

Rutter, M., Gillen, H. and Hagell, A. (1998), *Antisocial Behaviour by Young People*, Cambridge: Cambridge University Press.

Sanders, A. (1988), 'The Limits of Diversion from Prosecution', *British Journal of Criminology*, 28, p.513.

Scottish Office (1998), *Women Offenders - A Safer Way: A Review of Community Disposals and the Use of Custody for Women Offenders in Scotland*, Edinburgh: Stationery Office.

Singleton, N., Meltzer, H., Gatward, R. with Coid, J. and Deasy, D. (1999), *Psychiatric Morbidity Among Prisoners*, London: HMSO.

Social Exclusion Unit (1999), *Bridging the Gap*.

Tarling, R. (1993), *Analysing Offending: Data, Models and Interpretation*, London: HMSO.

Vaughan, P. (1999), 'Psychiatric Support to Mentally Disordered Offenders within the Prison System', *Probation Journal*, 46, 2.

Von Hirsch, A., Bottoms, A., Burney, E. and Wikstrom, P. (1999), *Criminal Deterrence and Sentencing Severity: An Analysis of Recent Research*, Oxford: Hart Publishing.

Von Hirsch, A. (1993), *Censure and Sanctions*, Oxford: Clarendon Press.

Von Hirsch, A. (1976), *Doing Justice: The Choice of Punishments*, New York: Hill and Wang.

Wasik, M. and Von Hirsch, A. (1988), 'Non-Custodial Penalties and the Principles of Desert', *Criminal Law Review*, pp.555.

Woodbridge, J. and Frosztega, J. (1998), *Recent Changes in the Female Prison Population*, London: Home Office.

Wolfe, T. (1999), *Counting the Cost: The Social and Financial Consequences of Women's Imprisonment.* London: Prison Reform Trust.

Woolf, H. and Tumim, S. (1991), *Prison Disturbances April 1990*, cm1456, London: HMSO.

Worrall, A. (1997), *Punishment in the Community: The Future of Criminal Justice*, London: Longman.

Worrall, A. (1981), 'Out of Place: Female Offenders in Court', *Probation Journal* 28 (3), pp 90-93.

Zedner, L. (1994), 'Reparation and Retribution: Are They Reconcilable?', *Modern Law Review*, 57, pp 228.

Appendix A
Terms of Reference

PRISON REFORM TRUST
COMMITTEE ON WOMEN'S IMPRISONMENT

Terms of reference

Bearing in mind: (i) the record number of women in prison, and
                     (ii) the record growth in the number of women prisoners;

To consider the use of imprisonment for women offenders, and ways of reducing the reliance upon custody;

To consider, in particular, the treatment of women defendants and offenders with mental health problems;

To consider the present structure of the women's prison system, and ways of ensuring that women prisoners are held close to their homes;

To consider the rules and regulations under which women's prisons are run, and the degree to which they reflect women's special needs;

To consider the treatment of mothers and babies in prison;

To consider issues relating to the imprisonment of women foreign nationals;

To consider the resettlement of women prisoners on release;

To consider any other matters that the Committee may consider relevant;

To make such recommendations as the Committee may think fit, along with a timetable for their implementation;

To report within 18 months of being established

Prison Reform Trust
15 Northburgh Street
London EC1V 0JR   revised: November 1997

Appendix B
People and Organisations who Submitted Evidence to the Committee

Frances Ablitt – Inner London Probation Service
Professor Dr. Hans-Jorg Albrecht – Max Planck Institut
Helen Allen - Greater Manchester Probation Service
Mary Blackburn – National Advisory Council of Boards of Visitors for England and Wales
Christopher Boothman – Commission for Racial Equality
Laura Camfield – Female Prisoners' Welfare Project
Professor Pat Carlen – University of Bath
Emma Cluley – University of Sheffield
Angela Devlin. – writer and broadcaster
Russell Dobash – University of Manchester
Rona Epstein – CAB, Warwickshire
Diana Fulbrook - Warwickshire Probation Service
Lucy Gampell – Federation of Prisoners' Families Support Groups
David Gillman – Babies in Prison
Nicola Hammond – Offenders and Corrections Unit
Susan V. Hartshorne.
Olga Heaven – Female Prisoners Welfare Project and Hibiscus.
Professor Roger Hood – University of Oxford Centre for Criminological Research
Dr. Sebastian Kraemer and Maggie Cohen – The Whittington Hospital
Sally Malin – Catholic Agency for Social Concern
Dr Aleka Mandaraka-Sheppard – University College London
Marjory Martin – Derbyshire Probation Service
Mike Nellis – Crime and Community Justice Committee of Britain Yearly Meeting (the Religious Society of Friends)
Ken Norman – The Portia Trust
Mike Octigon - West Midlands Probation
Brendan O'Friel.
Ann Power - Greater Manchester Probation Service
Jenny Roberts – Hereford and Worcester Probation Service
Professor Paul Rock – London School of Economics
Rene van Swaaningen – Erasmus Universiteit Rotterdam
Maeve Sherlock – National Council for One Parent Families
Frances Simon – Brunel University
Dr. David Thomas Q.C. - Institute of Criminology, University of Cambridge
Linda Thomas – LMT Consulting
Dr Jane Woodrow
Dr Ann Worrall – Keele University

Appendix C
Attendance at Seminars held by the Women's Committee in February 1999

Sentencing and the Custody of Women Offenders
Chris Boothman - Commission for Racial Equality
Professor Pat Carlen (speaker) - University of Bath
Angela Devlin - writer and broadcaster
Anita Dockley - Howard League for Penal Reform
Lucy Gampell - Federation of Prisoners' Families Support Groups
*Chandra Ghosh
Mary Groom – Co-Secretary, Committee on Women's Imprisonment
Helena Kennedy QC (speaker)
Janet Harber - Federation of Prisoners' Families Support Groups
Dave Hartley - Hazelwood House
*Lesley Harvey
Stephanie Hayman - Kings College, London
Dr Norman Hindson - Associate Specialist, Hazelwood House
Mrs Hodges - HMP Cookham Wood
Liz Hogarth - Senior Probation Officer at HMP Holloway
Rekha Kodikara - representing Paul Flynn MP
*Professor Nicola Lacey
Chris Lewis (speaker) - Home Office Research and Statistics Directorate
Ann Mace - Chief Probation Officer, W.Yorks Probation Service
Madeleine Moulden - Governor of HMP Styal
Mike Octigon - West Midlands Probation Service, Pre-Trial Services
Owen Roland - Women's Policy Group, Prison Service
*Elaine Player
*Wendy Rose
Stephen Shaw - Prison Reform Trust
Clare Sparks - Co-Secretary, Committee on Women's Imprisonment
Julia Stephens-Row - Association of Chief Officers of Probation
Chris Tchaikovsky - Women in Prison
Linda Toovey - HMP Bullwood Hall
*Professor Dorothy Wedderburn
Dr Anne Worrall - Keele University

Mental health problems and the needs of women offenders
Patricia Allison - Board of Visitors at New Hall
Sarah Carter - Hazelwood House
Louis Blom-Cooper
Angela Devlin – writer and broadcaster

*David Faulkner
Myra Fulford - The Bourne Trust
*Jane Geraghty
Roberta Graley
Mary Groom – Co-Secretary, Committee on Women's Imprisonment
Angela Hall - The Bourne Trust
Dave Hartley - Hazelwood House
*Lesley Harvey
Norman Hindson - Hazelwood House
Rekha Kodikara - representing Paul Flynn MP
Sue Kesteren NACRO Mental Health Unit
Dr Sebastian Kraemer - Consultant in Child and Family Psychiatry, Whittington Hospital
*Professor Nicola Lacey
Zena Labounkova - Senior Medical Officer, HMP Holloway
Nancy Loucks
Mrs Lynch - Board of Visitors at HMP Cookham Wood
Liz Mayne - Women in Special Hospitals (WISH)
Heather Monroe - ACOP Policy Development Officer
Susan Ngan - Bates, Wells and Braithwaite
Jill Peay - Law Dept, London School of Economics
Dr Mary Piper (speaker) - Healthcare Directorate, Prison Service
*Elaine Player
Susan Raven
*Wendy Rose
Baroness Ruth Runciman
Nicola Singleton (speaker) - Office for National Statistics
Clare Sparks - Co-Secretary to Committee on Women's Imprisonment
Dr Pamela Taylor (speaker) - Institute of Psychiatry
Julie Traynor - National Schizophrenia Fellowship
Crispin Truman - Director, Revolving Doors
Gill Walker - Board of Visitors at HMP Send
*Professor Dorothy Wedderburn
Yvonne Wilmott - Women's Policy Group, Prison Service
Toby Wolfe - Researcher, Committee on Women's Imprisonment

Community Sentencing and Alternatives to Prison
Frances Ablitt - Camden Women's Centre
David Atkinson - Dorset Probation Service
Helen Cash
Emma Clueley - Inner London Probation Service
Ann Dickinson - Merseyside Probation Service
Jane Dominey - Cambridgeshire Probation Service
Myra Fulford - The Bourne Trust

*Jane Geraghty
*Chandra Ghosh
Mary Groom - Co-Secretary to the Committee
Sue Hanley - West Midlands Probation Service
Susan V Hartshorne
Lord Hurd (speaker) - former Home Secretary and Chair of Prison Reform Trust
*Professor Nicola Lacey
Jackie Lowthian - Women Prisoners' Resource Centre
Professor George Mair (speaker) - Liverpool John Moores University
Mary Mitchell - Devon Probation Service
Sue Morton - HMP Cookham Wood, Probation
Sue Nicholson - Ripon House Probation Hostel
Colin Pinfold - Leicestershire and Rutland Probation Service
Ann Power - Greater Manchester Probation Service
Penny Privett - Board of Visitors - HMP Send
Margaret Putnam - Inner London Probation Service
Jenny Roberts - Hereford and Worcester Probation Service
*Wendy Rose
Judith Rumgay (speaker) - London School of Economics
Christine Scally - Cheshire Probation Service
Stephen Shaw - Director, Prison Reform Trust
Professor Joe Sim - Liverpool John Moores University
Clare Sparks - Co-Secretary, Committee on Women's Imprisonment
Caroline Stewart - Women's Policy Group, Prison Service
*Professor Dorothy Wedderburn
Mrs West - Board of Visitors, HMP Cookham Wood

The Social, Political and Economic Context of Women's Imprisonment
Francis Ablitt - Camden Women's Centre
Dr Silvia Casale
Angela Devlin – writer and broadcaster
Chris Duffin - Prison Reform Trust
Nick Flynn - Prison Reform Trust
*Chandra Ghosh
Linda Hartley - West Midlands Probation Service
*Lesley Harvey
Stephanie Hayman - Kings College, London
Professor Frances Heidensohn - Goldsmiths College, London
Professor Barbara Hudson (speaker) - University of Northumberland
Linda Jones - Head of Women's Policy Group, HM Prison Service
Rehka Kodikara - representing Paul Flynn MP
*Professor Nicola Lacey (speaker)
Mrs McCann - Board of Visitors at HMP Cookham Wood
*Wendy Rose

Stephen Shaw - Director, Prison Reform Trust
Clare Sparks - Co-Secretary, Committee on Women's Imprisonment
Professor Betsey Stanko - ESRC Violence Research Programme, Brunel University
Chris Tchaikovsky - Women in Prison
Paul Tidball - Governor, HMP Drake Hall
Peter Tiffin - Board of Visitors HMP Send
*Professor Dorothy Wedderburn
Peter Winkley - Governor, HMP Eastwood Park

* Denotes a member of the Committee on Women's Imprisonment

Appendix D: Counting the Cost

We commissioned a study by Toby Wolfe, an Oxford economist to examine the total costs of imprisonment. He attempts to estimate not simply the direct costs incurred by HM Prison Service but the wider costs to local authorities and probation services of children in care etc, and also takes account of such things as the savings to social security while women are in prison. The full report gives a detailed account of all the issues which should be considered in an analysis of costs and benefits:

- Provides evidence of orders of magnitude.

- Notes some of the difficulties involved in attaching monetary values to non-monetary consequences.

- Reports some of the attempts which have been made to attach monetary values.

Copies of the full report *Counting the Cost: The Social and Financial Consequences of Women's Imprisonment* (February 1999) may be obtained from the Prison Reform Trust. Here we reproduce Toby Wolfe's executive summary, together with the description of the basis for his financial calculations and some tables which serve to illustrate orders of magnitude.

Counting the Cost:
The Social and Financial Consequences of Women's Imprisonment

Executive summary

When magistrates and judges choose whether or not to imprison women offenders, their decisions can have far-reaching social and financial consequences. The financial costs imposed on the government are extremely large. And there may be dramatic social consequences, for the families of offenders, for the level of employment, for the level of crime and the fear of crime across the community, and, of course, for the offenders themselves.

While the financial costs of imprisoning women are similar to those of imprisoning men, the social consequences of imprisoning women are distinctive and may be more damaging. In particular, it is in the impact on families – above all children – that we see the harmful effect of imprisoning women. This report attempts to count the cost of women's imprisonment.

Consequences are not the only grounds on which magistrates and judges should make their decisions, and this report makes no attempt to recommend any particular policies. But there are certain groups of women prisoners for whom it is clear that there are plausible alternatives to prison, and this report compares the consequences of imprisonment for these women with the consequences of alternatives:

- Many women who are currently given short custodial sentences (say, up to six months, or up to 12 months) could be given community penalties (such as probation orders, community service orders, or curfew orders). For the community penalties to be proportionate to the crimes committed, they could be of long duration, and with additional requirements such as residence in a probation hostel.

- Many women who are currently remanded in custody after their arrest – before they are tried and/or sentenced – could be given bail, possibly with some condition attached, such as residence in a bail hostel or participation in a bail support scheme.

- Many foreign nationals who are currently deported at the end of prison sentences – typically long prison sentences imposed for drug importation – could be deported immediately, instead of serving a prison sentence.

The full report contains an extensive bibliography and list of sources used in making the financial estimates.

Decisions to place such women in prison may have the following social and financial consequences:

Financial costs to public bodies

The financial cost to public bodies of keeping the number of women in prison at its current level is extremely large – something like £118 million every year. The bulk of this is direct costs to the Prison Service, principally the costs of operating prison establishments, but also overheads and capital costs. There are a number of other financial costs – such as child care by local authorities, post-release supervision by the probation service, and lost tax revenues. There are also some financial benefits for public bodies – arising from a reduction in the level of crime and reduced payments of State benefits. But the direct cost to the Prison Service is so large that it dramatically outweighs the other financial costs of imprisonment, and is very likely to outweigh the financial benefits.

- The average cost of a 6-month sentence for a woman prisoner is £9,500, while that for a 12-month sentence is £18,600. This is considerably more than the cost of most community penalties. The average costs of different community penalties lie in the range £1,800 to £3,000. Where community penalties are made onerous, and in particular where residential requirements are added, the cost difference between them and custody is much smaller. Taking account of the cost of crime reduces the cost differential further. But the financial cost of a short prison sentence is still likely to be higher than the cost of a community penalty.

- The average cost of remanding a woman in custody is £4,800. The cost of bail is considerably lower. There is minimal cost involved in bail without conditions. A bail support scheme on average raises the cost of bail to £700, and a residential requirement on average raises the cost to £1,300. Remanding a woman in custody may reduce the number of crimes committed, but the financial benefit is unlikely to outweigh the high costs to the Prison Service.

- The cost to public bodies of a custodial sentence for a foreign national can be extremely high. The cost of a 6-year sentence for heroin importation is about £120,000. Immediate deportation would save the entire sum.

We can estimate the full financial cost of imprisoning these three groups of women. If we make a number of plausible assumptions, and follow through the financial implications of the scenarios above (that all the women currently given short prison sentences be given community penalties, that a proportion of the women currently remanded in custody be given bail, and that foreign nationals be deported without serving a prison sentence), we can estimate that there might be a financial saving to public bodies of something like £40 million every year.

Social consequences

It is difficult to quantify many of the social consequences of women's imprisonment, and it is even more difficult – if not foolish – to place monetary values on them. For this reason, it is hard to compare these social consequences with the financial costs to public bodies. They are an altogether different type of 'cost' – they are human costs, rather than financial costs. Nevertheless, the scale of the social costs is clearly such that the financial costs only tell a fraction of the story:

Children's living arrangements

45 per cent of women in prison had dependent children living with them at the time they were imprisoned. Imprisoned mothers frequently experience difficulties making arrangements for the care of their children. Whereas the majority of the children of *male* prisoners remain in the home and are looked after by their other parent, this is the case for only 5 per cent of the 8,100 children affected each year by the imprisonment of their mother.

The large majority of dependent children are looked after by relatives or friends while their mother is in prison, and in the large majority of cases this involves the children leaving home. Siblings are quite often separated between different substitute-carers. Child-care may impose a significant financial burden on carers and can cause considerable disruption to their lives. The difficulties experienced by substitute carers often result in children being moved from one carer to another while the mother is in prison, and sometimes result in local authorities being asked to look after the children.

About 8 per cent of dependent children are taken into local authority care subsequent to their mother's imprisonment, either when she first enters prison or during her sentence. Most are looked after by foster parents, but a significant minority are placed in children's homes. It can take time for mothers to regain care of their children after their release from prison, particularly where they are unable to obtain secure housing (see below).

Family life

Nearly 25 per cent of women in prison were lone parents before their imprisonment. In such cases, the household is fully broken up as a result of imprisonment – children are looked after elsewhere, and homes are often lost.

In other cases, while the household may remain intact, it nevertheless comes under great stress. It is not uncommon for relationships to break down under the strain of imprisonment. Households may suffer from the loss of valuable domestic work, child-care, and, in some cases, informal care of the sick, handicapped or elderly. Households may also lose an important source of income.

After release, women face an initial period of considerable stress in which they have to rebuild their family lives: they may have to find new employment, new housing and even new possessions, they may have to rebuild damaged relationships, and they may face a struggle with local authorities to win back care of their children. It may take time for prisoners to become 'deinstitutionalised', and they may experience difficulties being reintegrated into their families. Foreign nationals from some cultures face extreme difficulties as a result of the stigma that is attached to women's imprisonment.

All these difficulties are compounded by the financial difficulties faced by many women on release. Many prisoners leave prison more in debt than they were at the time of imprisonment, and the financial support available from the government to tide ex-prisoners through the first weeks after release is rarely sufficient. Some feel the financial strain on release is so great that they have little alternative but to reoffend.

Housing

One third of women prisoners lose their homes while in prison and are forced to find new accommodation on release. Many of these cases arise because women in prison for longer than 13 weeks lose their entitlement to any housing benefit and are often evicted because of non-payment of rent. Some other cases may result from broken relationships.

The loss of a home often results in a loss of possessions. When a woman is evicted while she is in prison, her possessions are typically thrown away.

Many of those who lose their homes move to temporary or insecure housing on release from prison. Some women have nowhere else to go and leave prison homeless. If they do not have children, they are unlikely to be regarded as priority cases by local authorities and may not be re-housed. Even if they do have children, they may only be offered temporary accommodation by the local authority.

Employment and unemployment

Roughly 30 per cent of women prisoners previously had jobs and were made unemployed as a result of imprisonment. In addition, economic theory suggests that a reduction in the labour-force reduces the overall level of employment, and thereby reduces economic output. The labour-force is reduced not only by imprisoning women who would otherwise have been employed, but also by imprisoning women who would otherwise have been *seeking* work – a further 20 per cent of women in prison.

All these women face difficulties in gaining employment on their release from prison. There is strong evidence that employers prefer not to hire ex-prisoners.

Had they been given community penalties or been bailed, most of the women in work could have retained their jobs. In addition, those given community service orders or combination orders carry out voluntary work for the benefit of the community.

Mental and physical health of the prisoner

While prison is not a healthy environment for anybody, there is some evidence that it has a very damaging effect on many women. Women prisoners are more likely than male prisoners to report suicidal thoughts, suicide attempts, self-harm and depression while in prison. After release, women suffer further from the disruption to family-life that prison often causes, and from social stigma. Suffering among mothers may be damaging not only to the mothers, but also to their children.

Prison may be a particularly inappropriate environment for the many women who are already suffering from mental illness when they enter prison. Women are twice as likely as men to report having received help for mental or emotional problems in the year before coming to prison. Such prisoners confront an environment that is particularly ill-suited to their recovery.

Many women prisoners have drug habits on entering prison, but it is unclear how prison affects drug use in the long run. While drug use is common within prisons, availability is lower than outside prison. However, many women go straight back onto drugs upon release, and there is a particular danger of overdose as ex-prisoners attempt to return to their previous levels of drug use.

The well-being of children

All the factors discussed above may have a very harmful impact on the well-being of children. Children may have several changes of carer and they may be looked after by people they do not know, they may feel rejected, they may witness strained relationships, they may lose their homes, their mothers may suffer depression and financial hardship. Even very short periods of imprisonment can be distressing and confusing to children.

What is more, children have little opportunity to visit their mothers in prison, and visits are often made difficult by the length of the journey, particularly for women prisoners, who (because of the geographical spread of women's prisons) tend to be further removed from their families than male prisoners. Visits are particularly difficult where women are foreign nationals and their families live abroad.

There is clear evidence that children's well-being is harmed in the short-term. While their mothers are in prison, children often suffer behavioural and emotional problems.

There is also some evidence of long-term harm. Many of the children of imprisoned mothers become delinquent in later youth and go on to suffer more general disadvantage. Of course, the mother's imprisonment is by no means the only explanation – these children often come from backgrounds of poverty, unstable parental relationships, insecure housing, periods in and out of care, criminal fathers, etc. The concept of 'social exclusion' expresses the way in which these and other forms of disadvantage are often found clustered together. But the mother's imprisonment contributes to many of these factors, and – importantly – prison may be a wasted opportunity to look for more creative solutions to address the root causes of social exclusion.

Crime

It is sometimes argued that a socially *beneficial* consequence of imprisonment may be that it reduces the number of crimes committed, through 'incapacitating', reforming or deterring the person imprisoned, or through deterring others. However, evidence suggests that only the incapacitation effect is significant, and even with that effect the impact may not be large.

Imprisonment does physically restrain some offenders from committing crimes they would otherwise commit – it 'incapacitates' them. But there are a number of reasons why the effect may not be large, especially for women. Firstly, not all offenders are repeat-offenders, and the evidence suggests that women are less likely to reoffend than men. Secondly, some measures outside prison can incapacitate offenders to a degree, in particular penalties with residential requirements and electronic tagging. Thirdly, even when in prison, offenders can commit certain offences, and offences can be committed on their behalf by those outside prison (e.g. theft in order to pay for drugs which are then smuggled into prison).

There is no evidence that the imprisonment of women is more effective than community penalties in the rehabilitation or deterrence of the individual, or in deterring others. There is no overall difference between prison and community penalties in their impact on reoffending. And the evidence on general deterrence indicates that potential offenders respond to changes in the likelihood that they will be caught and punished, but not to changes in the severity of punishment they are likely to face. Giving community penalties to some women who are currently given prison sentences would probably have little impact on the number of crimes committed.

Fear of crime

It may be argued that the 'general public' feels more secure if offenders are put in prison rather than being given community penalties, and that this is a socially beneficial consequence of imprisonment. However, opinion surveys suggest that public support for imprisonment may largely reflect a misperception of the current use of imprisonment and a desire for retribution, rather than a belief that prison is effective in reducing crime.

Conclusions

- If women who are currently given short prison sentences were instead given community penalties, all the harmful social consequences discussed above would be avoided, and few beneficial consequences would be lost.

    – If prison sentences for women were simply made *shorter*, all the social consequences of imprisonment would remain. However, some of the social costs (and the social benefits) would be smaller in scale.

- Remanding women in custody gives rise to nearly all the social consequences which prison sentences give rise to. The only differences are that women remanded in custody are less likely to lose their homes and may face less social stigma, and that women tend to be remanded in custody for relatively short periods of time (although it can be for long periods).

- Where foreign nationals are imprisoned, the social consequences discussed above may be extreme. Foreign nationals typically receive long prison sentences, are far removed from their families, and sometimes face extreme social stigma.

Part B: Counting the cost

Having explored the wide range of social consequences of women's imprisonment, it is now possible to draw these together in order to assess:

1. the full financial costs to public bodies of imprisoning women;

2. the social costs and benefits of imprisoning women; and finally

3. the social costs of imprisoning women in comparison with those of imprisoning men.

Financial costs to public bodies[2]

The financial cost to public bodies of keeping the number of women in prison at its current level is extremely large – something like £118 million every year (see table B1 on page 110). The bulk of this is direct costs to the Prison Service, principally the costs of operating prison establishments, but also overheads and capital costs. The direct financial costs of prison places are so large that they dramatically outweigh the other financial costs of imprisonment, and are very likely to outweigh the financial benefits arising from a reduction in the level of crime (on this, see also Prison Reform Trust 1998).

The particular groups of women prisoners on which this report focuses account for a large proportion of this sum. Women serving sentences of 12 months or less cost public bodies about £26 million every year (**Table B2**), of which women serving sentences of 6 months or less account for about £15 million every year (**Table B3**). Women remanded in custody cost about £29 million (**Table B4**). Foreign nationals with deportation orders cost about £17 million (**Table B5**). Added together, the financial cost of imprisoning these groups of women is more than half the total financial cost of women's imprisonment.

It is difficult to estimate what the financial saving for public bodies would be if these groups of women were not put in prison. There are, for example, many community penalties available, there is considerable cost variation between them, and it is impossible to know what proportion of today's prisoners might instead be given each of the alternatives. Any estimate of total financial savings must therefore rely on a number of assumptions. Before attempting such an estimate, it is useful to consider the possible range of costs which might be incurred for individual women given alternatives to custody.

A woman with a short prison sentence

● The average cost of a 6-month sentence for a woman prisoner[3] is £9,500 (**Table B6**), while that for a 12-month sentence is £18,600 (**Table B7**).

● The cost of most community penalties is considerably lower. Excluding the

2   It must be stressed that most of the figures given here are very approximate indeed, and are intended only to indicate orders of magnitude.

3   There is of course no such thing as the 'average' woman prisoner. Women in prison have very varied social circumstances and personal characteristics. The social costs associated with an individual depend heavily on whether she has children put in care, whether she was previously in the labour force, whether she loses her home, whether she is a repeat-offender, etc.

cost of crime, the average cost of a CSO is £1,800 (**Table B11**), of a curfew order is £2,900 (**Table B12**), and of a probation order is £3,000 (**Table B9**). Where community penalties are made onerous, and in particular where residential requirements are added, the cost difference between them and custody is much smaller. The maximum length of CSO may cost £2,400 (**Table B11**), the maximum probation order may cost £6,300 (**Table B9**), and a long probation order with a residential requirement may even cost more than a six-month custodial sentence (**Table B10**).

● Adding the cost of crime reduces the cost differential further. On average, a single offence costs public bodies something like £1,200. A six-month custodial sentence would therefore be cheaper than an average CSO if it prevented seven or more offences, and it would be cheaper than an average probation order if it prevented six or more offences. Similarly, a 12-month custodial sentence would be cheaper than an average CSO if it prevented 15 or more offences, and it would be cheaper than an average probation order if it prevented 14 or more offences.

In considering the likelihood of this many offences being prevented by a short prison sentence, two factors should be borne in mind. First, only three months of a six-month sentence will actually be served in prison, and only six months of a 12-month sentence. Second, some community penalties limit the number of crimes which are committed. They may do this through a degree of incapacitation, as well as through deterrence and rehabilitation.

A woman remanded in custody

A similar comparison may be made for a woman currently remanded in custody:

● The average cost of remanding a woman in custody is £4,800 (**Table B8**).

● The cost of bail is considerably lower. Excluding the cost of crime, there is minimal cost involved in bail without conditions. A bail support scheme on average raises the cost of bail to £700, and a residential requirement on average raises the cost to £1,300 (**Table B13**).

● Taking into account the average cost of crime to public bodies, remanding a woman in custody would be cheaper than bail if five offences were prevented as a result of the 42 days on average spent on remand. A residential requirement reduces the likelihood of offences being committed while on bail, but its expense means that only three offences would have to be prevented by custody to make custody cost-effective.

A woman due for deportation at the end of her prison sentence

When one turns to consider a foreign national due to be deported at the end of her sentence, the issue becomes much more clear-cut:

- The cost to public bodies of a custodial sentence for a foreign national can be extremely high. The only significant costs are prison operating costs, overheads and capital. The cost of a 6-year sentence for heroin importation, with no time spent in open prisons, is about £120,000 (3 × £39,500 = £118,500).

- Immediate deportation would save the entire £120,000.

Estimate of possible financial savings

If we make the following assumptions (which are intended to err on the side of over-estimating the costs of alternatives to custody):

– that, of women currently serving sentences of 12 months or less, 2/5 are given probation orders, 2/5 are given CSOs, and 1/5 are given curfew orders;

– that those currently given sentences of six months or less receive community penalties of average duration, while those given 6-12 months receive penalties of maximum duration;

– that residential requirements are added to half of probation orders, with three months residence for those currently given sentences of six months or less, and six months residence for the others;

– that half of women currently remanded in custody are bailed, half of these with residence requirements and the other half on bail support schemes; and

– that all the foreign national women currently given prison sentences with deportation orders are given immediate deportation orders,

then, while public bodies might save £56.5 million every year through a reduction in the prison population,[4] they would have to spend £16.5 million every year on alternatives for these women.[5] There might therefore be a possible financial saving of £40 million every year. In addition, expenses might be incurred which would be associated with an increase in the number of crimes committed. It is difficult to estimate how many additional crimes would be committed, but the number may not be large, and the cost they impose on public bodies is unlikely to approach £40 million every year.

Social consequences

Part A of this report demonstrated the importance of broadening our 'calculations' to include the social consequences of women's imprisonment. But Part A of the full report also demonstrated the difficulty of quantifying many of these consequences, let alone of placing monetary values on them. For this reason, tables B14, B15 and B16 are limited to lists of the relevant categories of cost with some explanatory notes, and readers are referred back to Part A of the full report for more detailed discussion of the order of magnitude of each social cost.

4 This figure = cost of imprisoning women with sentences of 12 months or less (£25.6 million) + half the cost of all women remanded in custody (£14.3 million) + the cost of all foreign national women with deportation orders (£16.6 million).

5 This figure is based on the cost estimates in tables B9 to B13 and on the reception data cited in the full report. The additional expenditure on alternatives would be (666 × £3,000) + (146 × £6,300) + (666 × £5,700) + (146 × £11,800) + (1,332 × £1,800) + (292 × £2,400) + (812 × £3,000) + (1,280 × £1,300) + (1,280 × £700) = £16.5 million.

Table B14 clearly illustrates how the consideration of social costs dramatically alters the nature of any cost-benefit analysis of women's imprisonment. There are a large number of social costs which result from the imprisonment of women, and as the discussion in section A made clear many of these social costs are large.

A woman with a short prison sentence

- Table B14 is based on a comparison of a short custodial sentence with a community penalty. Where a woman is given a community penalty instead of a short custodial sentence, all of the social costs listed in the table are avoided.

- It is perhaps foolish to compare the size of these social costs with the financial costs to public bodies. They are an altogether different type of 'cost' – they are human costs, rather than financial costs. Nevertheless, the scale of the social costs is clearly such that the financial costs only tell a fraction of the story.

- There is only one significant social *benefit* of imprisonment – the effect of incapacitation in reducing the number of crimes committed. There is considerable uncertainty as to the number of crimes avoided by imprisoning women and the number may not be large (although it will clearly be greater than zero). Placing a monetary value on this incapacitation effect is particularly hard if social costs are being included. The average social cost of a single offence has been estimated at £3,000, but this figure must be treated with extreme caution. What is more, even if this figure is plausible, the social benefit of fewer crimes cannot be straightforwardly measured against the social costs listed in table B14. Nevertheless, the discussion in Part A of the full report suggests that, while the incapacitation effect may not be large, many of the social costs clearly are large.

- If, instead of moving women away from prison onto community penalties, prison sentences for women were simply made *shorter*, all the social costs of imprisonment listed in table B14 would remain. The only difference would be that many of the social costs would be smaller in scale. For example, (unlike with community penalties) women would still face difficulties making child-care arrangements, although they would be separated from their children for a shorter period of time. Or, in terms of housing, while shorter prison sentences would mean that a larger proportion of women would be entitled to retain their housing benefit for the duration of their time in prison, it would still be the case (unlike with community penalties) that many women would lose their homes. Shorter prison sentences would also have the effect of reducing the social benefit of imprisonment through incapacitation.

A woman remanded in custody

An 'R' in the central column in table B14 indicates that a particular social cost (or social benefit) of a custodial sentence also results from remanding a woman in custody. The social consequences of remand are compared with the social consequences of bail.

The social cost-benefit analysis for women on remand is similar to that for women given custodial sentences:

● Remanding women in custody gives rise to a large number of social costs, though slightly fewer than is the case for a custodial sentence.

● Since remand is typically for a short length of time, some of the social costs are small in scale, but they still remain. It should also be remembered that some women are remanded in custody for long periods.

● The fact that remand is typically for a short period of time also reduces the size of the one social benefit of remand (the incapacitation effect).

A woman due for deportation at the end of her prison sentence

The social cost of giving long custodial sentences to foreign nationals before deporting them is extreme. As noted above, the financial costs of long prison sentences are in themselves very high. To these must be added a range of social costs, listed in table B15. The magnitude of many of these costs may be considerably greater than in the case of British nationals.

Comparing men and women

Finally, table B16 compares the social costs of imprisoning women with the social costs of imprisoning men:

● The differences in *financial* costs are minimal. Some are larger in the case of men, and some in the case of women, and in no case is the difference large.

● Turning to the wider *social consequences*, however, there are many more costs associated with the imprisonment of women, and it is reasonable to suppose that, when considered together, they are considerably larger than those associated with the imprisonment of men.

In no sense is this meant to suggest that the social costs of imprisoning men are not large. On the contrary they can be extremely large. But – in answer to the tasks set in the Introduction to this report – the social costs of imprisoning women are quite distinctive, they may be significantly larger than those for men, and they may be large even when compared with the substantial direct costs of imprisonment incurred by the Prison Service.

110

B1: Women's imprisonment – annual cost to public bodies

Cost category	Notes		Sum
Prison operating costs	£24,500 x 3,100 places		£ 75,950,000
Prison overheads & capital	£12,600 x 3,100 places		£ 39,060,000
less health care costs	*less* 5% of operating costs	less £	3,798,000
Post-release supervision	Total supervsn. costs of probation service (0.1372 x £409.4 mill) times proportion of the prison population that is female (4.75%)		£ 2,671,000
Lost tax revenues	18 % of total lost output (£ 12,720,000)		£ 2,290,000
less lower State benefits	*less* 52 weeks @ ((360 x £62) + (670 x £104)) per week	less £	4,784,000
Local authority Child Care	For further details, see full report		£ 6,197,000
			£117,586,000
TOTAL	Round to nearest £1 million		**£ 118 million**

B2: All sentences ≤ 12 months – annual cost to public bodies

Cost category	Notes		Sum
Prison operating costs	£24,500 x 680 places		£ 16,660,000
Prison overheads & capital	£12,600 x 680 places		£ 8,568,000
less health care costs	*less* 5% of operating costs	less £	833,000
Post-release supervision	£250 x 530 female young offenders discharged after sentences of ≤ 12 months.		£ 133,000
Lost tax revenues	680/3,100 x (18 % of total lost output (£ 12,720,000))		£ 502,000
less lower State benefits	*less* 52 weeks @ ((130 x £62) + (100 x £104)) per week	less £	960,000A
Local authority Child Care	For further details, see full report.		£ 1,550,000
			£ 25,620,000
TOTAL	Round to nearest £1 million		**£ 26 million**

B3: All sentences ≤ 6 months – annual cost to public bodies

Cost category	Notes		Sum
Prison operating costs	£24,500 x 380 places		£ 9,310,000
Prison overheads & capital	£12,600 x 380 places		£ 4,788,000
less health care costs	*less* 5% of operating costs	less £	466,000
Post-release supervision	£250 x 430 female young offenders discharged after sentences of ≤ 6 months.		£ 108,000
Lost tax revenues	380/3,100 x (18 % of total lost output (£ 12,720,000))		£ 281,000
less lower State benefits	*less* 52 weeks @ (130 x £62) per week	less £	419,000
Local authority Child Care	For further details, see full report		£ 1,022,000
			£ 14,624,000
TOTAL	Round to nearest £1 million		**£ 15 million**

B4: All remands in custody – annual cost to public bodies

Cost category	Notes	Sum	
Prison operating costs	£26,900 x 700 places		£ 18,830,000
Prison overheads & capital	£12,600 x 700 places		£ 8,820,000
less health care costs	less 5% of operating costs	less	£ 942,000
Lost tax revenues	700/3,100 x (18 % of total lost output (£ 12,720,000))		£ 517,000
less lower State benefits	less 52 weeks @ (230 x £62) per week	less	£ 742,000
Local authority Child Care	For further details, see full report.		£ 2,119,000
			£ 28,602,000
TOTAL	Round to nearest £1 million		£ 29 million

B5: All foreign nationals with deportation orders – annual cost to public bodies

Cost category	Notes	Sum	
Prison operating costs	£26,900 x 420 places		£ 11,298,000
Prison overheads & capital	£12,600 x 420 places		£ 5,292,000
			£ 16,590,000
TOTAL	Round to nearest £1 million		£ 17 million

B6: 6 month sentence – average cost to public bodies

Cost category	Notes	Sum	
Prison operating costs	£24,500 / 4 (assuming she serves only 3 months in prison, i.e. $1/4$ of a year)		£ 6,130
Prison overheads & capital	£12,600 / 4		£ 3,150
less health care costs less	5% of operating costs	less	£ 310
Post-release supervision	£250 x proportion of women prisoners discharged after sentences of £6 months who are young offenders, i.e. 15% (in 1997, 430 out of 2,850 – Home Office 1997a, pp.68 & 94).		£ 40
Lost tax revenues	$1/4$ of (18 % of £4,100 per prisoner-year)		£ 180
less lower State benefits	less $1/4$ of (£419,000 (see table above) / 380 per prisoner-year)	less	£ 280
Local authority Child Care	45% chance of having 2.1 children, 8% of whom incur costs of (£3,200 + (85% x 3 months @ £184 per week) + (15% x 3 months @ £1,100 per week) + £650)		£ 610
			£ 9,520
TOTAL	Round to nearest £100		£ 9,500

B7: 12 month sentence – average cost to public bodies

Cost category	Notes	Sum	
Prison operating costs	£24,500 / 2 (assuming she serves only 6 months in prison, i.e. ½ a year)		£ 12,250
Prison overheads & capital	£12,600 / 2		£ 6,300
less health care costs	*less* 5% of operating costs	less £	610
Post-release supervision	£250 x proportion of women prisoners discharged after sentences of ≤ 12 months who are young offenders, i.e. 15% (in 1997, 530 out of 3,520 – Home Office 1997a, pp.68 & 94)		£ 40
Lost tax revenues	½ of (18 % of £4,100 per prisoner-year)		£ 370
less lower State benefits	*less* ½ of (£960,000 (see table above) / 680 per prisoner-year)	less £	710
Local authority Child Care	45% chance of having 2.1 children, 8% of whom incur costs of (£3,200 + (85% x 6 months @ £184 per week) + (15% x 6 months @ £1,100 per week) + £1,300)		£ 970
			£ 18,610
TOTAL	Round to nearest £100		£ 18,600

B8: Remands in custody – average cost to public bodies

Cost category	Notes	Sum	
Prison operating costs	£26,900 x (42 out of 365 days)		£ 3,100
Prison overheads & capital	£12,600 x (42 out of 365 days)		£ 1,450
less health care costs	*less* 5% of operating costs	less £	150
Lost tax revenues	42/365 of (18 % of £4,100 per prisoner-year)		£ 80
less lower State benefits	*less* 42/365 of (£742,000 (see table above) / 700 per prisoner-year)	less £	120
Local authority Child Care	45% chance of having 2.1 children, 8% of whom incur costs of (£3,200 + (85% x 42 days @ £184 per week) + (15% x 42 days @ £1,100 per week))		£ 390
			£ 4,750
TOTAL	Round to nearest £100		£ 4,800

B9: Probation order (with average additional requirements)

	Average duration (17 months)	Maximum duration (3 years)
Costs to probation service	£ 2,400	£ 5,100
Costs to other agencies (est.)	£ 70	£ 150
Breach costs @ 20% (est.)	£ 480	£ 1,030
Additional crimes committed	• £1,200 cost to public bodies per crime • £3,000 social cost per crime	
TOTAL	**> £ 3,000**	**> £ 6,300**

B11: Community service order

	Average duration (122 hours work over 0.7 of a year)	Maximum duration (240 hours work over 1 year)
Costs to probation service	£ 1,100	£ 1,500
Costs to other agencies (est.)	£ 30	£ 50
Breach costs @ 60% (est.)	£ 660	£ 900
Additional crimes committed	• £1,200 cost to public bodies per crime	
TOTAL	**> £ 1,800**	**> £ 2,400**
Including social costs / benefits:		
Additional crimes committed	• £3,000 social cost per crime	
less community service work	Less £ 440	Less £ 860
TOTAL	**> £ 1,400**	**> £ 1,600**

B12: Curfew order

	Lower estimate	Higher estimate
Costs to probation service	£ 1,750	£ 1,900
Costs to other agencies (est.)	£ 50	£ 60
Breach costs @ 60% (est.)	£ 1,050	£ 1,140
Additional crimes committed	• £1,200 cost to public bodies per crime • £3,000 social cost per crime	
TOTAL	**> £ 2,900**	**> £ 3,100**

B13: Bail[5]

	Notes	*Sum*
Bail	Minimal costs	–
Bail with residence in a hostel	42 days @ £30.28 per day	£ 1,300
Bail with bail support	42 days @ £110 per week	£ 700
Additional crimes committed	• £1,200 cost to public bodies per crime • £3,000 social cost per crime	

---

5   If it is the case that people tend to spend longer on bail than they do on remand (Netten & Knapp 1992, p.11), then the figures in this table are under-estimates.

B14: Social costs and benefits of women's imprisonment (when compared with community penalties)

	R = also remand	Notes
Social costs:		
Financial costs to government	R	Difference between a short prison sentence (£9,500 for 6 months, and £18,600 for 12 months) and a community penalty (£1,800 to £11,800); or between remand (£4,800) and bail (£0 to £1,300).
Lost earnings from employment	R	For a 6-month sentence: Lost output – reduced tax payments = $\frac{1}{4}$ of 82% of £4,100 per prisoner-year = £800. For a 12-month sentence: Lost output – reduced tax payments = $\frac{1}{2}$ of 82% of £4,100 per prisoner-year = £1,700.
Separation from children	R	
Substitute carers	R	Financial difficulties and burden of work and responsibility
Distress to children	R	
Social exclusion	R	Greater likelihood of inter-generational transmission of social exclusion
Strains on family life	R	
Household work	R	Loss of work within the household, both domestic work and informal care of adults
Employment	(R)	Stigma among employers, whereas community penalties can sometimes improve employability and community service benefits the community
Housing		Frequent loss of home and possessions
Financial difficulties	R	Especially on release
Social stigma	(R)	
Psychological harm to the prisoner	R	
Social benefits:		
Incapacitation	R	Possibly £3,000 per crime prevented

B15: Women with deportation orders – social costs of imprisonment

Social costs:	
Financial costs to government	£120,000 for a 6-year sentence
Separation from children	Extreme
Substitute carers	Financial difficulties and burden of work and responsibility
Distress to children	Possibly even greater than for British nationals
Social exclusion	Greater likelihood of inter-generational transmission of social exclusion
Strains on family life	Extreme
Household work	Loss of work within the household, both domestic work and informal care of adults
Social stigma	Possibly extreme
Psychological harm to the prisoner	
Note: Low likelihood of a social benefit from incapacitation	

B16: Differences between men and women – the social costs of a 6 month prison sentence

Cost category	Notes	Sum (where quantifiable)
Social costs greater for the imprisonment of women:		
Prison operating costs	£6,100 for a woman. For a man: £20,000 / 4 = £5,000. (Assuming both serve only 3 months in prison, i.e. ¼ of a year). Difference = £6,100 - £5,000	£ 1,100
Local authority Child Care	45% chance of having 2.1 children, 8% of whom incur costs of (£3,200 + (85% x 3 months @ £184 per week) + (15% x 3 months @ £1,100 per week) + £650)	£ 600
Separation from children		
Substitute carers	Financial difficulties and burden of work and responsibility	
Distress to children		
Social exclusion	Greater likelihood of inter-generational transmission of social exclusion	
Strains on family life		
Household work	Loss of work within the household, both domestic work and informal care of adults	
Social stigma		
Psychological harm to the prisoner		
Incapacitation	Fewer crimes prevented by the imprisonment of women than by the imprisonment of men	
Social costs greater for the imprisonment of men:		
Lost output (lost earnings plus lost tax revenues)	For a woman: ¼ of (£12.72 mill / 3,100) = £1,000. For a man: the labour-force falls by 80% of total male prison places (62,194), i.e. 49,800. With NAIRU at 6%, employment falls 46,800 in long-run. Given lowest quartile male annual earnings of £13,800 (ONS 1998c, A28), this implies total lost output of £645.84 mill. So average lost output for a male prisoner with a 6-month sentence = ¼ of (£645.84 mill / 62,194) = £2,600. Difference = £2,600 - £1,000 = £1,600	£ 1,600
Reduction in State benefits	On average, the imprisonment of a woman for 6 months reduces benefit payments by £300. For men: total claimants fall by (NAIRU x approx. 80% of 62,194) + (approx. ½ of 20% of 62,194) = 9,200. Men serving ≤ months make up approx. 8% of all men's prison places (Home Office 1997a, pp.16, 23). So those serving 6 months reduce benefit claimants by 9,200 x 8% i.e. 740. Total benefit payments reduced by (52 weeks @ (740 x £57) = £2.2 mill. So each 6-month sentence reduces this by ¼ of (£2.2 mill / 4,735 prisoner-years) = £120. Difference = £300 - £120 = approx. £200.	£ 200
Employment	Stigma among employers, whereas community penalties can sometimes improve employability and community service benefits the community	